HOW TO COPE WITH DIFFICULT PEOPLE

An expert on the subject of difficult people, ALAN HOUEL holds an MA in Sociology and Communication, is a specialist in educational technology and in management psychology, and Assistant Director of the Centre for Business Development in Paris. Since the mid 1980s he has been conducting seminars on management training, communication and negotiation techniques for groups of national and multinational executives, in Europe and South America.

CHRISTIAN GODEFROY is a specialist in positive thinking and auto-suggestion. He has given training seminars to over 6,000 senior company personnel around the world on self-confidence, communication and relaxation. Today he concentrates on publishing books about personal and professional success and about health and runs his own highly successful publishing companies in France and Switzerland.

D0179117

Overcoming Common Problems Series

Selected titles

A full list of titles is available from Sheldon Press,
36 Causton Street, London SW1P 4ST and on our website at
www.sheldonpress.co.uk

Overcoming Common Problems

HOW TO COPE WITH DIFFICULT PEOPLE

Alan Houel
with Christian Godefroy

sheldon **PRESS**

First published in Great Britain in 1994

Sheldon Press
36 Causton Street
London SW1P 4ST

© Original edition published by Edi Imer S.A. Switzerland
Represented by The Cathy Miller Rights Agency, London
© UK Edition: Sheldon Press 1994

British Library Cataloguing-in-Publication Data
A catalogue record for this book is available from the British Library

ISBN 0–85969–682–0

9 10 8

Photoset by Deltatype Ltd, Birkenhead, Wirral
Printed and bound in Great Britain by
Ashford Colour Press

Contents

Introduction

There are certain recurring situations in our lives – encounters that seem to follow the same pattern, which often involve difficult people. How many people do you know who complain bitterly about their employers, or who end up with a succession of divorces after living out a series of sadistic and destructive dramas? 'Maybe they'll be luckier next time', we say to ourselves, yet each time the story seems to repeat itself, and the relationship ends in disaster. What about you? Have you ever had to deal with an explosive boss? A maddeningly, unco-operative bureaucrat? A hostile client? An arrogant sales person? A moody, taciturn subordinate, a grumpy colleague? An apathetic, unruly student? If not, it's either because you live on a desert island, or because you're fooling yourself. Whatever the reason, if you've never had to deal with difficult people, then you don't need to read this book.

'I can't stand Charles any more!', a biologist mutters about a colleague. 'We're supposed to work together, but whenever I make a suggestion, he cuts me off, treats me like some kind of ignoramus, and gets angry if I insist on making my point. Of course, as soon as my back's turned, he starts talking as if the idea were his, and if it works, he takes all the credit. He never shares. He never discusses anything, even though we're supposed to have regular meetings. I don't know what to do any more.'

'I saw my father. It was a disaster', says a young man of twenty-five. 'He still doesn't take me seriously. In his eyes, I'm still a kid, an ignorant kid. He contradicts everything I say, and gets angry every time we try to have a discussion. He knows it all, and I don't know anything. He'll even stick to an opinion that he knows very well is totally contradictory, just so he won't have to admit I'm right. He gets upset and starts to complain about his health, and then I feel guilty for making him feel bad.'

How easy life would be if we didn't have to deal with difficult people! Relationships would be harmonious, and there would be more justice and tolerance in the world. Is there something we could do to get what we want, even from difficult people? Are there any secrets for making human relations harmonious and effective, however difficult people appear to be? Whether we're talking about day-to-day life, or about our

1

personal or intimate relationships, or about the family or about work, it's always useful to know how to deal with difficult people in order to communicate and live side by side as best as possible. By harmonizing our relations, we assert ourselves and develop our own personalities, while at the same time allowing others to do the same.

The Main Types of Difficult People

People who are difficult to deal with can be categorized into a few main types. You'll quickly realize you've been dealing with some of them on a regular basis. We'll start with an overview, and then examine each type in detail in the rest of the book, and how to deal with them.

The Aggressors

This category includes behaviours such as hostility, the desire to hurt, being sarcastic, refusing to co-operate, arrogance, and a know-it-all attitude. The aggressive person tries to dominate, will not hesitate to resort to insult, and, contrary to popular belief (their bark is worse than their bite), will not hesitate to stab you in the back if it serves their interests. Such people are self-appointed experts, who, because of their pride, refuse to admit they may not know all there is to know.

The Complainers

You're familiar with the complainers, grouches, and other negative types – there are sure to be a few among the people you know. According to these people, the only thing life has to offer is bad luck. Their principal characteristic is that they love to complain – finding a solution to their miseries would eliminate their primary reason for living! Their only mission seems to be to throw a bucket of cold water on anyone who demonstrates enthusiasm for anything. The problem is that their attitude is toxic: their illness is contagious – and therefore dangerous.

The Clams

This final type consists of a particular form of invertebrate who either say nothing, or at best talk about the weather – without ever saying what they think or feel. Such people limit their communication to grunts and groans. On a particularly good day you may get a yes or a no out of them.

Dealing with Difficult People

Don't be discouraged if you regularly seem to be confronted with difficult people. There are a number of methods for dealing with these kinds of situations. You can attain your objectives without resorting to force. You have a number of 'weapons' at your disposal, the effectiveness of which will astonish you, once you learn how to use them.

Inner Shields

The first condition for successfully dealing with difficult people is to make yourself impermeable. The difference between someone who is vulnerable and someone who appears indestructible is the latter's ability to construct inner shields. Below are a few pointers on how this can be done.

Words. Whether to defend yourself or support your point of view, you can learn to use words skilfully and make them your ally. We'll be looking at the principles of using words effectively later on.

Negotiation. This is an art, yet your daily life is a succession of transactions which are open to negotiation. Later we'll show you how to come out a winner in your transactions with difficult people.

Humour. This can be a powerful weapon, used to take the drama out of a situation, and to temper your aggressive feelings. It can defuse a lot of bombs, and get you out of many a lion's den without a scratch.

1

What Are You Made Of?

You enter a room full of people. Conversation stops, heads turn your way. People recognize you, and say hello. Some come up smiling and shake your hand, others get on with their discussions. You walk around, then stop to chat with an acquaintance.

A scene like this depends on two elements which are interdependent, and which form your personality: the image you project through your physical appearance, voice, handshake, and gestures. The second element is your personality, which is a dimension of your self that is much more difficult to pinpoint than your image.

In theory, your image should simply be a reflection of your personality. But you know very well this usually isn't the case! Anyone can modify their image more or less successfully. Because we try to present as favourable and flattering an image of ourselves as possible to the outside world, you should never rely entirely on image to judge a person's personality – the two can be diametrically opposed. When we have nothing to go by except a person's image, it's very difficult to make anything more than a superficial judgement of a person.

Four Forces that Determine Your Personality

Your personality is made up of myriad factors, which haven't been fully identified by psychologists, and which are regularly the subject of ferocious controversy. Nevertheless, it is useful to know about the four main forces that combine to determine your personality: emotional needs, economic needs, models and values.

Your Emotional and Economic Needs

If you were raised in a warm and loving atmosphere, you're more likely to expect other people to like you, and you are never stingy with your affection. Similarly, if you were raised in an economically privileged environment, you're much less likely to become a miser. However, if you were raised in a family that didn't demonstrate much affection, this doesn't mean you're incapable of feeling or expressing love – it just means you may find it more difficult to love yourself and others. Neither does this mean that because you earned your money with the sweat of your brow and were poor as a child that you automatically become a miser. Far from it! But your attitude towards the privileged classes is likely to differ from that of a person born with a silver spoon in his/her mouth.

If you were always encouraged and supported in your endeavours, whatever they may have been, then you probably have a good measure of self-confidence. You know your worth, you're aware of your intellectual capacities, and you certainly don't fall into the category of perpetual victim. On the other hand, if the people who were important in your life always put you down, or had no faith in your intellectual ability, then you probably make a perfect victim for difficult people. You have trouble asserting yourself, and you always try to appear above the situation – without necessarily succeeding.

Your Models

The models you choose for yourself, either consciously on unconsciously, also exercise an important influence on the way you behave. In early childhood, you probably modelled yourself after one of your parents, and unconsciously imitated him or her. A little later on, you may have chosen a friend, or a teacher with whom you had a close relationship, or a famous personality, or a colleague, a superior, a partner, and so on.

Your Values

Your values are formed by your education, your environment, your studies, job, travels, your religious convictions and your conception of right and wrong.

Are You Able to Assert Yourself?

This point is very important. Evaluating your capacity for self-assertion will dictate how you orient your training. The following exercise will help you to make an honest evaluation of yourself. To have a reasonable discussion with a difficult person, you must know how to assert yourself, and you must also be aware of your weak points so you can protect yourself. The people you judge to be difficult may not be considered so by others: 'objectivity' is a word which doesn't exist in the vocabulary of human relations.

Questionnaire: Are You Self-Affirming?

Answer the following questions by circling either yes or no.

1. Do you believe other people are straightforward YES   NO
and honest with you?

2. Are you able to laugh at yourself?   YES   NO

3. Can you list five people who had a strong influence   YES   NO
– either positive or negative – on your life?

4. Do you consider yourself honest with others?   YES   NO

5. Do you think it's a good idea to list your faults and   YES   NO
qualities?

6. Are you interested in analyzing yourself and your   YES   NO
life?

7. Are you often disappointed by others?   YES   NO

8. Do you think total control of your emotions is   YES   NO
necessary in order to assert yourself?

Comments

Give yourself one point for each correct response.

1. Yes. It's important that others are honest with you. Even though the truth isn't always pleasant to hear, it's an important step on the road to maturity and self-affirmation. If you're under the impression that people around you are afraid of telling you the truth, then you're probably one of those difficult people who make human relations such a sticky business!

2. Yes. Most psychologists agree that being able to laugh at yourself means you know yourself, and that you can judge yourself without resentment.

3. Yes. We're all influenced by other people. If you answered no, then you're not being honest with yourself. You refuse to recognize the influence of the people you associate with, and it's possible you fall into one of the categories of difficult people, either the aggressive type or the know-it-all (see Chapter 2). Take the time to draw up a list of people who influence you – it's an excellent exercise.

4. Yes. If you insist on people being honest with you, then the least you can do is return the favour.

5. Yes. Make two lists: one of your qualities and one of your faults. Then ask someone who knows you well and whose judgement you respect for their opinion. If you can't think of anyone to ask, it may be a sign that you're not completely honest with yourself.

6. Yes. If you aren't, then you may wake up one day to find your life has lost its meaning, that you live to work instead of work to live, and that your personal relations have become simple habits.

7. No. Of course we are occasionally disappointed by others, but we should always ask ourselves if we're not trying to shift the blame on to someone else's shoulders, or if we are seeing ourselves as we really are.

8. No. It's neither realistic nor healthy to spend your time trying to master your emotions. Among other things, you lose contact with yourself. For example, if you know that a given situation irritates you, you'd try to avoid it. On the other hand, if you recognize your need for affection and satisfaction, you should try to fill this need. You will become a more fulfilled person, whom others will want to know.

Results

0–2: You don't see yourself as you are. Other people may perhaps find you hard to deal with. You will not be able to assert yourself, become a fulfilled person, or gain the upper hand when dealing with difficult people if you don't reconcile the way you see yourself with the way you really are.

3–5: You have certain moments of lucidity. Unfortunately, you don't take the time to evaluate yourself seriously. Make the effort – success is at your doorstep.

6–8: You know yourself, you're honest with yourself, and you're probably honest with others as well. You will need only minimum effort to learn how to deal successfully with difficult people. You are mature and prepared to accept what life has to offer – happiness and sadness, joy, success, and failure.

Are You the Prey of Difficult People?

As you've noticed, some people never complain about others. For them, there's no such thing as a difficult person. They seem to have a great talent for human relations, and are surrounded by people who show great affection and admiration for them. As well, these privileged persons always seem to know exactly what to say to resolve unpleasant situations. *How do they do it?*

These talented people have the ability to instil all their personal relations with a quiet efficiency. They are confident and fulfilled, and fear neither rejection by nor the hostility of others. Are you a member of this privileged group? If you're not sure, complete the following test by circling either yes or no.

Questionnaire: Are You Quietly Efficient?

1. Do you talk about your accomplishments in order   YES   NO
to impress people?

2. Do you have trouble saying no?   YES   NO

3. Do you feel your partner doesn't understand you?   YES   NO

4. Are you easily affected by other people's bad   YES   NO
moods or depressions?

5. Do you find it difficult to be alone or private   YES   NO
without feeling guilty?

6. Do you have trouble distancing yourself from   YES   NO
people who you find boring or unpleasant?

7. Do you tend constantly to justify yourself?   YES   NO

Results

Each 'yes' represents an aspect of your behaviour that you should work on. If you don't, you'll continue to fall prey to difficult people. For them, you're a perfect victim: they consider you to be a weak person, which makes upsetting you a lot easier!

Accept Yourself as You Are

David is a stockbroker who lost his job a year ago when his company was bought out by a large corporation. He hasn't been able to find another job since then: every time he goes to a job interview something happens – he immediately feels dislike for the person sitting across the table, and loses all his self-confidence. When David tried to contact old business acquaintances to see if they could help him, they all seemed eager to escape as quickly as possible – even before he'd had the chance to ask for their support.

A few sessions with a personal development counsellor opened David's eyes to a lot of things. He understood that he alone was responsible for his situation. Lacking self-assurance and confidence, he felt a constant need to reassure himself by boasting, name-dropping, and annoying his listeners with exaggerated accounts of his exploits. Unfortunately, no one was taken in, and David became a victim of his own lack of self-love. No wonder he didn't do well at job interviews!

If you want to assert yourself in order to come out a winner in your encounters with difficult people, you have to learn to accept yourself as you are. If you want to maintain fruitful relations with others, the first condition for success is to stop communicating from a position of inferiority – so heed the following advice!

Avoid Getting Upset

If you find somebody's behaviour shocking, ignore it – especially if you're not directly involved. By showing your outrage, you adopt the attitude of a victim, and automatically place yourself in an inferior position. If you allow yourself to be manipulated on an emotional level, you won't be able to gain the upper hand when confronting difficult people. Whenever you feel irritated by the attitudes of people who have no real influence on your life, shrug them off. Learn to say 'So what?' to yourself.

Exercise: Developing Serenity and Self-Confidence

- For the next few days, write down any events, attitudes, or behaviour which you find shocking or insulting.
- Analyze each event. To what degree did your attitude work in your favour? Be completely honest with yourself.

As the exercise gradually becomes part of your daily routine, you'll notice you're less affected by events which you previously found outrageous or disconcerting. You will acquire more self-confidence and a sense of inner serenity – and your blood pressure will go down!

Improve Your Appearance

As far as human relations go, the first few minutes of contact are often decisive in determining the future of the relationship. Even though we know appearances are often deceptive, it is a fact that many relationships are either formed or abandoned because of appearance.

Also, appearance is important in developing self-esteem. You will be less likely to assume the role of victim if you are well groomed, if you create the impression you're someone who takes care of yourself and feel good about your physical appearance. *Remember: you have no chance of coming out on top if you show signs of inferiority right at the start.*

Exercise: Appraising Your Appearance

1. What do you think about the way you look right now?

2. Make a list of what you like and don't like about yourself.

I like:

I don't like:

3. Now, how would you try to enhance your positive aspects, and diminish your negative ones?

To enhance my positive aspects I would:

To diminish my negative aspects I would:

Are your clothes right for you? If you're not sure, ask for advice. If you know someone who is thought to have good taste, you'll flatter them by asking – as a bonus, you may gain a friend, as well as good advice about clothes.

Learning to Say No

Let's face it, it's much harder to say no than to say yes. If you're honest with yourself you'll admit you've often said yes when you wanted to say no: you have to work over-time on a night you're supposed to go out with your spouse – but you don't dare say no to your boss; you agree to babysit for a friend on Saturday night, when you'd really prefer to do something on your own; and so on. And each time you say it won't happen again.

Fear of Rejection

The motivating force behind an inability to say no is very often a fear of rejection. This fear, however, is not a real threat: you don't lose a friend's affection or respect just because you refuse to do something for him or her. If this does happen, the person didn't merit your affection – and even less your respect – in the first place!

Always saying yes when you really want to say no will make you bitter and cause you unnecessary stress. If you want to affirm yourself and deal successfully with difficult situations, you must learn to say no, tactfully, politely, and gently – but also firmly. You'll be respected, and you may discover that people who you previously found difficult become easier and easier to handle.

Exercise: *Learning to Say No*

For each of the following situations, choose the reply which you think is best.

1. Your mother-in-law calls and wants you to take her shopping on a Saturday afternoon. You would prefer staying home. You respond by saying:

    a. 'I'm really sorry, but I have a dentist's appointment.' (You don't really have an appointment.)
    b. 'I don't feel like shopping. I find it boring. I have more important things to do.'
    c. 'Would you mind if we postponed it for another afternoon? I really feel like I need to rest up this weekend.'

2. At the end of an exhausting day, your boss asks you to take some files home and study them that night. You reply:

    a. 'Really! I have better things to do with my evenings!'
    b. You make up some excuse.
    c. 'I'm too tired to do any useful work this evening. What if I do it on Saturday morning instead?'

3. Your partner invites someone over for dinner whom you can't stand. You say:

    a. 'All right, we'll let it go this time. But next time tell me in advance so I can make other plans.'
    b. You agree to entertain the person because you don't want to anger your partner.
    c. You go out yourself, and let your spouse entertain the guest alone.

Answers

1. The best answer is 'c'. It can be dangerous to invent excuses ('a'.), since you may be found out later, especially if you're dealing with someone you see frequently. 'B' is tactless, and borders on being rude; your mother-in-law would probably feel offended by it.

2. Once again, the best response is 'c', for the same reasons.

3. The best response is 'a'. You calmly make your position clear, while agreeing to the invitation one last time. You could also opt for the last response – leaving your spouse alone with the guest. That way everyone will probably have a better time, you included!

Become aware of similar situations that are likely to arise in your life, and make a list of possible responses. Little by little, you'll learn to say no.

2

Aggressive Types

'I'm so sorry, sir,' explains the sales person, 'but your guarantee has expired. Anyway, you can't blame the fact that your toaster isn't working on faulty production. You probably did something . . .'

'What! Is this supposed to be some kind of joke?' the client replies angrily. 'What kind of store is this! You sell defective items, and you have the nerve to call me a liar!'

'Not at all, sir. Try to calm down', mumbles the sales person. 'That's not what I was trying to say . . .'

'Ha! I know very well what you were trying to say! I want to talk to the manager! At least *he* may be a little more competent than you . . .'

'This presentation is a disaster', groans the vice-president, looking over sketches for an advertising campaign. 'The client will never approve it.'

'A disaster!' the art director in charge of the project exclaims indignantly. 'What are you talking about? We think it's just fine, and we came in under budget! Everybody thinks it's great.'

'Everybody? Who's everybody? You mean the group of idiots I have working for me? You're not even capable of making a decent presentation!'

'But sir . . .' the art director sputters.

'Get out of here before I get really mad! Go do this thing again!'

Difficult people are primarily aggressive, hostile, arrogant types – nicknamed 'steamrollers'. People in this category often seem to take issue not only with your behaviour or your reactions, but also with you as a person. They seem to be accusing you of just existing, and you may end up believing they dislike or even hate you, and that they have the right to verbally brutalize you because of their superior position.

When they discover just how much they can terrorize and humiliate their victims, as soon as they find themselves in positions of authority such aggressive types count on the effects their behaviour produces in other people.

People with dominating, antagonistic characters are very hard to live

14

and work with, both for the people around them and themselves. They're often angry, and are rarely able to share moments of simple pleasure. The only way they feel they can get something from another person is through threats and criticism.

What to Do When Faced with a Steamroller

In situations similar to the ones we've just described, you should adopt the following strategy.

Refuse to yield an inch of ground. Steamrollers have a good idea of how their behaviour is going to affect you; they're in the habit of intimidating others and getting what they want. If you stand up to their insults and hostility, you'll throw them off track. That's when you can take control of the situation, and suggest a more acceptable attitude. Let's take another look at the first scenario:

'What! Are you trying to make fun of me?', the client replies angrily. 'What kind of store is this! You sell defective items and then won't even admit it! And you have the nerve to call me a liar!'

'Not at all, sir', replies the sales person, calmly but firmly. 'You misunderstood me. If you'd care to leave your toaster with us, we'll call you as soon as we find out what's wrong with it, and give you an estimate for the repairs. If that's not satisfactory, perhaps you'd care to talk to the manager?'

The situation has been turned around, and the sales person has removed any grounds for hostility:

- by refusing to get upset or defensive, the aggressive client's insults disappear;
- by suggesting a simple and logical line of action, the sales person keeps the discussion in a realistic framework;
- by suggesting a meeting with the manager, the client is forced to think twice. If there were any blame or guilt in the matter, would the sales person suggest a meeting with the manager? Probably not. Also, the manager is much less likely to be intimidated than the sales person.

All the client can do is to accept the solution suggested by the sales person, or take the toaster and leave. In both cases, the sales person remains in control of the situation.

Give the other person a chance to calm down. It's sometimes impossible not to react when an aggressive person explodes or intimidates you. But to avoid adding fuel to the fire, you must let the person calm down, and then oblige them to justify their behaviour. Let's look at the second scenario:

'This presentation is a disaster', groans the vice-president. 'The client will never approve it.'

'Why not?' the art director calmly asks.

'Why? It's obvious! Even you should be able to see it will never work!'

'Exactly. I'd be very happy if you could explain in detail why you think the campaign is a failure, and especially why you think the client won't approve it. You have much more experience than we do. Take your time. I'll get us some coffee . . .'

Once again, the bomb has been defused. The art director, without in any way demeaning himself:

- forced the VP to justify his anger and negative opinion of the project;
- didn't get upset, at least not outwardly, by the VP's sarcasm.
- gave the VP a chance to cool off by going to get coffee. If the VP persists in being aggressive, he'll just look like a fool, especially if the art director remains calm. Aggressive persons don't like to appear foolish, any more than anyone else.

Look for a way to de-escalate. If you're dealing with a steamroller, you must at all costs look for a way to de-escalate the situation. If you respond to hostility with hostility, you'll only feed their aggressiveness. Steamrollers take pleasure in antagonism, but if you can find a way to agree with someone who systematically disagrees with everything, they will become disoriented – in order to disagree with you, they will have to disagree with themselves.

The Surgical Type

'From what I know of your husband, he's not the type to sit around moping while you're away', says a geologist to his female colleague while on a two-week field-trip.

'It doesn't surprise me in the least that you can't change a tyre', says a husband to his wife. 'Why should you be any different from any other woman?'

These kinds of statements are typical of surgical aggressive types, who take pleasure in cutting you to the quick, and then dig the knife in some more. Their incisive remarks may assume many forms: double meanings, sarcasm, jokes at the expense of a third person, and so on. For example, while one person in a group is expressing an opinion, the surgical type will try to catch your attention, rolling his/her eyes in disgust. Remind you of anyone you know?

Disguised Hostility

Not all aggressive types express their hostility openly, as Steamrollers do. People who disguise their hostility, and create a false impression by pretending to be friendly at first are much more dangerous. These people prefer more subtle methods of attack because in reality they are cowards. They never dare to be openly aggressive because they are afraid the other person may get angry. By being hypocritical, they can always argue that they didn't mean any harm. In this way they avoid having to confront hostility head-on – which is precisely what makes them vulnerable, as we'll see a little later. However, before such people are found out, they usually succeed in doing a lot of damage.

Surgical aggressors, for example, speak in quiet tones, often accompanied by a slight smile. Inside, they take great pleasure either in their victim's passive suffering, or in their confused emotional reaction to a simple phrase or gesture, which has cut right to the heart of the victim. Surgical aggressors are notorious cowards. They don't deserve your compassion. They are perfectly aware of the harm they cause. You must counter-attack: set your scruples aside and assert yourself – don't let yourself become a scapegoat.

What Strategy Should You Use?

You have two strategies to choose from, both equally effective. It all depends on what you know about the aggressor and finding the hole in their armour. Both strategies require a great degree of self-control because a cutting remark by a surgical aggressor can hurt a lot more than an explosive insult by a Steamroller. Let's see what our lady geologist could have done with her colleague's cutting remark:

'From what I know of your husband, he's not the type to sit around moping while you're away . . .'

'You're right about that', says the lady geologist. 'He's full of energy. He's got the garage to paint, and our son's room needs new furniture.'

In principle, this should be enough to stop the aggressor. However, she or he may insist, saying something like,

'That's not what I meant . . .'

To which she might reply, 'Really? Well what exactly do you mean?'

The aggressor is now cornered and has to come out in the open, which is precisely what these people can't stand doing, and which is why they always resort to underhanded attacks. They'll either change the subject, or try to get out of it by making a joke.

Let's look at the second example:

'It doesn't surprise me in the least that you couldn't change a tyre . . .'

To which the wife can counter by saying something like,

'Doesn't it? That's interesting. Let's discuss it. Come here and sit down. I find this fascinating – I could talk about it all day, couldn't you?'

The man will suddenly remember a thousand things he has to do, since his vicious little attack was disarmed so effectively.

The second manoeuvre is carried out in two steps. The first consists of treating the attack in an impersonal manner. This is the surest way to gain a victory. If you are confronting an expert in surgical aggression, it will allow you to:

- take time out before counter-attacking;
- regain control of your emotions (provoking an emotional response is one way your adversary scores points);
- deprive the aggressor of satisfaction, since the remark doesn't seem to bother you at all.

What could be more frustrating for an aggressor than to be faced with a robot instead of an emotional victim? You don't have to leave the scene – you can stay where you are. However, if the remark was especially nasty, or if you feel you have to take a stand once and for all, you can use your advantage to launch a final blow. Let's look at how this could work in practice:

'From what I know of your husband, he's not the type to sit around moping while you're away. . . .'

The colleague replies, 'The theory that all men start chasing skirts as soon as their wives turn their backs for a moment originated in being unable to accept the success of females and in seeking ways to gain revenge on all women. Do you fall into that category?'

The tables are turned – the aggressor is now on the defensive. To

18

continue the discussion would mean risking an outdated macho attitude. Let's look at the second example:

> 'It doesn't surprise me in the least that you couldn't change a tyre. . . .'

> The wife replies, 'The concept of women as being inferior seems to be prevalent among older men, especially those who are insecure about their intellectual and other abilities. But I'm surprised to hear something like that coming from you, dear!'

It's unlikely the husband will repeat the same kind of attack in the near future. . . .

A Final Warning

Before putting the strategies you've learned so far into practice, make sure you're really being confronted with hostility. Does this seem obvious? Well, it isn't. People who are not difficult or aggressive can be easily fooled by appearances. So before getting irritated by the behaviour of a person you've judged to be hostile or aggressive, ask yourself a few questions:

- How do other people react to their behaviour?
- Can their behaviour be justified, even though it's different from the way I'd act in identical circumstances?
- Are they just playing a role in order to get what they want?
- Are they just using the occasion to let off some steam?

Making these distinctions is important: if you can't differentiate between real aggression and behaviour which has nothing to do with you, you risk provoking hostility which will then be very difficult to control. For example, a female solicitor has spent a trying day in court, and comes home to find her partner hasn't prepared dinner. Her nerves are on edge, she's exhausted, but her professional training prevents her from venting her dissatisfaction on colleagues and superiors. Instead, she attacks her partner. Now if he doesn't understand that her hostility is due to the difficult day she has had at work, he will respond aggressively in turn, and an all-out conflict will develop, with wounds inflicted on both sides. So, make sure the steps you take are necessary. If not, you risk destroying or harming a relationship that is important to you.

Your Exercise Programme

If you want to acquire the habit of reacting correctly when faced with aggressive people, you have to practise. Being able to come up with just the right remark, to stay calm and avoid getting into arguments, isn't something you can learn overnight.

Exercise: Confrontation

Complete one of the following discussions each day, using the techniques you've learned. Come up with at least three or four responses for each discussion. Some examples of acceptable responses appear at the end of the chapter.

1. Mother to her daughter: 'If you had any respect for me, you wouldn't dress like that whenever I take you somewhere!'

Your response:

2. Client to the assistant manager: 'And you're telling me he's not here? After I've come 200 miles to see him! You knew I was coming this morning, and you couldn't even tell him? How can an idiot like you still find a job!'

Your response:

3. Adolescent to his/her father: 'Really, Dad, even you should be able to understand I need the car at least one night a week!'

Your response:

Exercise: Listening to Others

Keep a small notebook with you at all times and listen to the conversations around you. Whenever you overhear an aggressive person, write down what they say. Then, when you have some free time, complete the discussion as if you were the object of their aggression, applying the techniques you've learned.

Exercise: Keep a Journal

When we've been irritated by an aggressive person, it's often only much later that we think of a remark we could have used to put them in their place. Keep a journal of the discussions you have with difficult and/or aggressive people, using the following model:

Place and date:

Situation:

1. What the other person said:

2. How I replied:

3. How I should have replied:

Sample Response

1. Mother to her daughter: 'If you had any respect for me, you wouldn't dress like that whenever I take you somewhere!'

Possible responses:

'Mother, where did you get the idea that I don't respect you?'

'This idea of respect is very interesting. Let's talk about it some more . . .'

'Why do you think I don't respect you?'

2. Client to the assistant manager: 'And you're telling me he's not here? After I've come 200 miles to see him! . . . How can an idiot like you still find a job?'

Possible responses:

'Sir, I did give your letter to the manager. If you wish to make a complaint to the president of the company, I'll be happy to give you

21

his name and address. But maybe I could first explain why the manager is unable to see you today?'

'Sir, I feel terrible that you've had to travel all this way for nothing, but if you ask your secretary, you'll see that we tried to reach you this morning, when the manager found out he had to take care of an emergency. If you want to file a complaint with the president . . .'

3. Adolescent to his/her father: 'Really, Dad, even you should be able to understand I need the car at least one night a week!'

Possible responses:

'Are you trying to tell me that I'm different from all your friends' fathers? Maybe we could discuss it, if you have a moment. I'm interested to know exactly what you think about me.'

'It's natural for adolescents to think that everyone is ganged up against them. Would you like to talk about it some more?'

'Adolescents who aren't very mature seem to think the only reason their parents exist is to say no. I didn't think you fell into that category.'

3

Complainers and
Other Negative Types

'I know you live pretty far away, Martin, but it's important for the work we're doing here that you get to work on time in the morning. I'd really appreciate it if you made an effort to do so.'

'You put the entire responsibility on my shoulders. You know it's not my fault if I get here late. The bus is slow, there's usually a traffic jam . . . Why do I always get the blame when the others are just as much at fault? Before you started working here no one ever complained about my being late . . .'

Mutual blame, accusation, protestations of innocence, suggestions of injustice in the world – complainers aren't the most difficult of people, they don't provoke the mental confusion characteristic of aggressive types, and their comments don't hurt as much as the cutting remarks of a surgical type, but even the most kind and gentle of people end up not being able to stand them!

Complainers and other negative types are never satisfied. If you admire the way they look, they'll say something like, 'What you *don't* know is that my blood pressure's high enough to explode any moment . . .' and so on, in a flood of complaints that's impossible to stop.

Defeatists and Pessimists

You probably know people who always respond to a suggestion by saying, 'It'll never work. I'm sure it won't . . .' and whose lives are felt to be an interminable source of problems. For this person – the defeatist – everything unpleasant that happens is caused by others. Only luck can produce a favourable situation, and even then they may not be able to regard it as such.

Pessimists find comfort in pessimism and use it as a crutch to attract other people's attention. If you try to help a complainer or other negative type to get rid of their problem, they won't be grateful in the least, since what you're doing is taking away one of their reasons for living! The first thing they'll do is look for another one – something else to complain about!

Forever the Victim

Complainers and other negative types are experts at spreading the poison in their minds. Listen to this short conversation which might give you a feeling of *déjà-vu*:

'Till number two didn't total up right yesterday, Madeline. I was wondering if . . .'

'If you knew how careful I am when I do my totals, you wouldn't come complaining to me . . . And if you didn't let more than one person handle the cash, you wouldn't have these kinds of problems . . .'

'I know, Madeline. The accountant hopes to get a better system in place soon.'

'A better system? We don't even *have* a system! It's not my job to worry about things like this, but since you're accusing me . . .'

Using great skill, Madeline has deflected the blame back on to her superior. She was able to put him on the defensive, and avoid the subject of her own possible errors. Although this is not ideal for getting promoted – bosses don't like to admit they're at fault – Madeline did avoid assuming any responsibility for the situation. She always places herself in the role of victim. Although she's in no way responsible for the cash error, she is nevertheless a source of embarrassment to her boss since he can't tell her anything without provoking a scene – the slightest criticism is enough to send her sulking off like a beaten dog.

Destructive Influence

Complainers and other negative types exercise a destructive influence on the people around them, often without being aware of it themselves. Their presence in a working group can be catastrophic. For example, listen to a young biology teacher, recently hired by a private school:

'We only have one microscope for every six students. That gives you some idea of how poor we are in equipment. How am I supposed to teach my course without a microscope for every two students. We lack money, but every time I bring the matter up with the headmaster, I'm depressed for the rest of the week. His stock response to whatever suggestions I make for raising funds is, "No one would agree, it'll never work. We tried it a few years ago, without success." Maybe he's right . . .'

As you see, a negative attitude can easily become contagious and undermine the whole team's morale. That's the most dangerous thing about it. Nevertheless, although they do fall into the category of difficult people by draining our enthusiasm, our energy, and zest for life, negative persons don't deserve the same drastic treatment as we would accord a surgical aggressive type.

Helping Them – and You Too

Often these people act in good faith, and do not harbour any harmful intentions. Nothing positive will be achieved by verbally abusing them. The best solution is to open the door to the prison of passivity and futility they live in – and try to get you to live in as well – by refusing to get sucked in to their cycle of accusation–defence–accusation. If you can't do this, the only remaining course of action is to protect yourself against their influence by remaining indifferent, or getting away as soon as possible. Here's a strategy you can use.

What are their Grievances?

To do this, you first have to listen attentively. It's likely that if you have a complainer in your midst, no one has really listened to them for a long time. Let the person know you're interested, that you understand what they're talking about – show them you're receptive to their problems. For example, let's say your brother-in-law is always complaining about his wife's (your sister's) behaviour:

'. . . and then she tells me it's my fault the children are always tired. She says it's because we don't take a holiday. But I have too much to do at work. Not like her – her job is a lot less demanding than mine. I do what I can, but with the new boss . . .'

This is like a self-hypnotic speech the brother-in-law has been carrying on with himself for a long time. You have to interrupt the flow by doing something unusual. Raise your hand, and say something like:

'Hold on a minute! I want to understand exactly what the problem is. My sister says the kids are tired because you didn't go on holiday. You say you can't go because you have too much work to do, and on top of that you have a new boss to deal with. Is that about right?'

But be careful! At this point, two kinds of traps may be laid for you, which you absolutely must avoid falling into. First, understanding doesn't mean you're in agreement. Letting someone know you understand what they're saying doesn't mean you agree with them. If it did, you'd never be able to resolve the issue, since you'd be implying that you are to blame, which will probably lead to a new series of grievances. So avoid saying things like, 'You're right . . .' or 'I agree . . .', which may be the easiest way to put an end to the discussion, but which won't solve anything.

Second, at all costs avoid the persecutor–victim–saviour triangle. When someone complains, they automatically assume the role of victim: 'They did this to me . . . they're out to get me . . . they don't care about me . . .' The person's moaning always seems to have some exterior cause. Wherever there's a victim, there's a persecutor. Although the victim may not come right out and say it, *you* will be placed in the role of persecutor:

> 'The children are upset and hard to control these days because they don't see enough of you, and because they know they're not going on holiday . . .'

> 'You know very well I can't just stop working . . .'

You, in the role of persecutor, have succeeded in making the complainer feel bad, guilty and forced to justify himself.

This type of exchange leads directly to a cycle of accusation–defence–accusation, which goes nowhere except to make him feel like a victim in turn, and start a new round of bickering.

It can get worse if a third person enters the ring, because whenever there is a victim and a persecutor, there is a golden opportunity for someone to play the saviour! When you lend a sympathetic or compassionate ear to a negative type, you're setting yourself up in the role of saviour.

In the preceding example, we saw how your brother-in-law came to you and told you about his problems with your sister. You may be tempted to reply by saying something like; 'Of course I understand, and I'm going to talk to her about it.' And there you are, committed to a role which you will surely regret having assumed later on. Why? Because in a victim–saviour–persecutor triangle, the roles often get changed around. If you speak to your sister in the role of her husband's saviour, you may soon become a victim yourself, since she could tell you to mind your own business. Or, you may be cast in the role of persecutor – she will accuse you of siding with her husband. Or, you may end up completely confused and not knowing who to save. There aren't many of us who haven't fallen into this kind of trap. For your own good, and for the good of the people you're trying to help, it's essential to avoid this pitfall.

Suggest Other Options

Once you've accurately summarized the situation, analyze each grievance and suggest other possible courses of action. But be careful! You'll have to demonstrate your creativity and suggest a number of alternatives. The complainer must then make a decision. It's not for you to decide what the complainer should or should not do. All you want to do is offer choices. Also, if you really want to help the person break out of the cycle of complaining, make your suggestions realistic. To do this, you may have to find out more about the situation. Reformulate what you've understood so far in your own words, and ask a few specific questions. Taking our example, first show you understand the problem. Don't allow any more complaining. If you are familiar with the situation, get right to the solutions:

> 'Okay, you have a number of choices. You stay at home, and your wife and kids go away together; you decide your family's happiness is more important than pleasing your new boss; you refuse your wife's request, and make a great impression with the new boss.'

Or, you can suggest a more methodical technique that will force the person to make a choice:

> 'What you might do to make deciding easier is to take a sheet of paper and write down the advantages and disadvantages of each option. Then you can compare them, and make a decision.'

Becoming Aware of Responsibility

Let's look at the motives behind the complaints made by Joanne, a forty-year-old woman who lived through a period of deep emotional shock when she found out that her husband was having an affair with a woman ten years her junior, whom he'd met at work. A divorce took place very quickly, totally upsetting Joanne's life. She hasn't been able to regain her sense of equilibrium since. Three years later, Joanne is well established in her role of complainer. She confronts life as if she were the victim of some terrible drama. She feels lonely and abandoned. Her old friends and acquaintances don't want to see her, fed up with hearing the same old stories about how she was mistreated. Then comes the day when she runs into you or me . . . When we show an interest in finding out more about her, she winds up the old phonograph and tells her story. We can leave it at that, or we can recount our own tragedy (misery loves company), or we can prudently maintain our distance. But what if we want to help her? Here's how to proceed.

First, ask a question: 'Joanne, would you like to solve this problem?' The answer will certainly be yes, since complainers are suffering and want to stop, at least outwardly. They feel trapped because they don't know what to do. Of course, if Joanne says no, leave me alone with my suffering, then it would be useless to continue. But if she agrees, there's no reason not to try:

'If you want to put an end to this, you'll have to answer my questions with complete honesty. Ready? Here's the first question: how do you blame yourself for your husband's leaving you?'

Joanne is speechless. She's just explained how she's the innocent victim, and here you are asking her to take responsibility! She looks around nervously, playing for time – after all, she did promise to answer honestly. Finally, she says, 'Really, I didn't want him to leave me!'

You continue. 'All right, you didn't want it. But in some ways you may have encouraged it to happen. Put a little oil on the fire when things were going badly, perhaps?' Joanne is pensive. She reviews the events of her divorce. She starts to see how she might have been at least partly to blame for the divorce. But she can't accept it yet.

Now you can say something like, 'All right, but why did you let him leave, if you wanted so much to keep him?' Watch Joanne's face – you'll see the curse that's been haunting her and condemning her to a life of solitude lift away. Her face lights up . . . 'You're right! I *was* happy when he left, the bastard . . .' And your work is done.

Leave Joanne alone with her thoughts for a few moments. She is starting to see the divorce from a different perspective, where she no longer has to play the role of victim. The danger here is if she says, 'Yes . . .' and goes on to come up with new rationalizations for playing the old, sad song. But with a little skill on your part, you can help her to invent a new version of events, where her role is more positive and attractive. This is what she has to do to liberate herself – and you've given her the opportunity to do so!

If things go well with Joanne, we can ask her to do the following:

'You say you felt happy that he left. Try to remember what you might have done to encourage or provoke his leaving. For now, just set aside everything that isn't your responsibility, and tell me about the divorce as if it were your doing.'

If Joanne is able to do this, it means she's liberated. It may be difficult for her since she has been so strongly attached to the old version of events, but for her own good insist she continues. Get her to tell you the story the way *you* want to hear it, and stop her at the slightest tendency to relapse into a complaining mode, and correct her immediately. In this way Joanne will rebuild her self-image and become a person capable of causing changes in her relationship. Although she may have been responsible for a negative change in the past, she can also initiate positive changes in the present.

Helpless or Responsible?

There are many ways in which we conceive our place in the universe. One is to see ourselves as a miniscule point in a vast and powerful universe, with no control of any kind. According to this philosophy, I can do nothing to change what happens to me, whether it's good or bad. I'm a prisoner in the flow of history – crushed by crises in the economy, threatened by urban violence, worn down by age. What can I do? Nothing! For example, I'm late because: the weather was so bad; there was a traffic-jam; my wife forget to get more petrol after she used the car; I had a flat tyre . . . and so on. People who are chronically late have amazing imaginations. They are the innocent victims of climactic, social, or mechanical forces beyond their control. This is how they keep a clean conscience. But the price they pay for hiding behind such arguments is much higher than they imagine: what they're admitting is that they have no power over themselves or over the environment in which they live. If they don't even have the power to arrive on time, they don't have the power to do anything that could improve their existence.

One of the ways people condemn themselves to a life of impotence is to abandon the power of being themselves by obeying commands of which they are not aware. These commands are often prohibitions, which were learned at a very early age and which have been completely forgotten. Nevertheless, these commands continue to exert a powerful and constant influence on their behaviour. Such commands include things like, 'Be perfect! Be nice! Be polite! Be strong (men don't cry . . .)! Be fast! Work hard!' A sign that someone is under the influence of such commands is when they have the habit of starting sentences with 'I should . . .', 'I have to . . .' You'll notice these phrases a lot in the way complainers and other negative types express themselves, for example, 'I have to get up every morning . . .' 'I have to go to work . . .' 'I have to put up with my clients' moods . . .' 'I have to put on a happy face . . .'

Becoming Creative

To help a negative person, whether it's you or someone else, you have to enable them to adopt a different understanding of their place in the universe. They must become aware that they have some weight, and are capable of standing on their own two feet. It's true we are surrounded by forces beyond our control, but it's also true that we exercise immense power on ourselves and on our environment.

You have the choice of seeing yourself as powerful and responsible, or impotent and irresponsible. To help negative persons first you have to help them to assume responsibility for what they do, and for the consequences resulting from their actions. To do this, use the following method.

Complainer: 'I have to get up every morning and go to work . . .'
You: 'What would happen if you didn't get up one day?'
Complainer: 'My boss would give me hell.'
You: 'And if you didn't go to work for a few days, what would happen then?'
Complainer: 'I'd get sacked.'
You: 'And if you lost your job, then what would happen?'
Complainer: 'I'd have a lot of trouble finding another job . . .'
You: 'And if you weren't able to find a job, what would happen?'
Complainer: 'My wife would probably leave me. They'd cut off the electricity . . . the phone . . . I'd have to move out of my house . . . I'd end up living on the streets like a tramp.'
You: 'And what would happen if you lived like a tramp?'
Complainer: 'I'd be very unhappy.'
You: 'So if I understand correctly, if you decided not to get up in the morning you'd become a tramp, and you'd be very unhappy?'
Complainer: 'Right.'
You: 'So you prefer getting up in the morning to being a tramp?'
Complainer: 'Yes.'
You: 'Then you get up in the morning because you *choose* to!'

The tables are turned. If a person *chooses* to do something instead of feeling obliged to do it, they become the master of their destiny – and can no longer play the role of victim. You can expect seasoned complainers to keep arguing that they are still obliged to do something even after you help them to realize they choose to do what they do in order to avoid unpleasant consequences, or to obtain substantial benefits. Don't be taken in by these arguments. Instead, ask the question: 'Is there anyone pointing a gun to your head? And even if there were, wouldn't you prefer to die rather than do something you find unacceptable?' Examples of persons choosing this extreme option are numerous, which demonstrates that we can remain in control of our destiny and be responsible for our choices, no matter what situation we find ourselves in.

Last Resort: Get Them Mad!

If in your charitable efforts to help a negative person all the above methods fail, then you can decide not to see them again, or to see them as seldom as possible in order to protect yourself against their negative influence. Defeatism is contagious, and you have every right to take care of yourself. You don't owe them anything, just because they happen to be victims and you're all right. Don't forget the persecutor–victim–saviour trap described earlier. If, however, you are not in a position to avoid the person – say they are a close relative or a colleague, or someone you refuse to abandon – a final assault is still possible. Don't forget there are hidden resources in everyone, even when they seem irretrievable.

As we've seen, complainers and other negative types are low-energy people; they walk around as if they were carrying a huge weight on their shoulders. Don't expect a hardened negative person to suddenly become highly motivated. What are they supposed to do – forget all the gross injustices and tragedies they've had to bear up to now?

Getting angry is a sign of progress for these people. It means helping them to shake off the weight that is crushing them, and to rebel against what they believe is their destiny. They'll experience a surge of energy – misdirected of course – which is much better than the passive existence they've been trapped in for so long.

Provoke them so their anger is directed at you. This can be done by challenging what they say, and the way they say it. Don't let them get away with using words and phrases that enhance their image of impotent victim – systematically insist they specify exactly what they mean, and help them to alter their perception of events so they assume responsibility for their lives. The worst that can happen is that the person gets mad at you – and even that would constitute some progress! Let's listen to John:

John: 'It's always the same old story. Every time we visit her parents, we have to sit and listen to them put us down. Everyone knows it isn't my fault. I'm discouraged, and I feel nobody gives a damn about me . . .'

As you listen, interrupt him every time he says something that isn't exact:

John: It's always the same old story . . .'
You: 'Always? Really, always? Hasn't there been just one time when it was different?'

Of course there has. Nobody is always the same, so you insist that John reformulate the statement by saying: 'Very often . . .' or 'Nine times out of ten . . .'

Next you help the person to concentrate on the positive side. Having established the possibility of saying something like, 'And what about the time it wasn't the same . . . what happened then?' you force the person to concentrate on the positive aspects of the situation.

Then, make sure the person uses 'I', the first person. This is an important step towards assuming responsibility for their actions.

John: '. . . that we go and visit . . .'
You: 'We? Who's we?'

31

John: 'I have to sit there and put up with . . .'
You: 'You have to? Who says you have to? What would happen if you didn't?' [And you continue with the method 'I have to . . . I choose to . . .' described earlier].
John: 'But everybody knows that . . .'
You: 'Everybody? But who exactly?'

At this point the person, if they haven't already exploded, will say something like . . . 'Who exactly? I don't know . . . *me*! That's who!'

Now you can ask: 'You? Well how do you know?' This forces the person to come up with the facts.
John: 'It isn't . . .
You: 'What do you mean by "it"?'

The person has to explain what 'it' means. The bad relationship with the parents? His own impotence to influence the situation, to be accepted by them?

John: 'I'm discouraged . . .'
You: 'Discouraged by what? By whom?' [Once again, insist on concrete facts.]
John: 'I get the feeling nobody gives a damn about me . . .'
You: 'Nobody? Really nobody? Isn't there anybody in the whole world who appreciates you just a little?'

Honesty will force the person to admit that you, at least, must like him since you're giving him so much of your precious time and attention! He will have to reformulate the sentence and say something like, 'I get the feeling a lot of people don't like me . . .' Even then, you should insist he reveal who exactly he thinks doesn't like him.

As you can see, this method of asking questions is powerful. A complainer who is challenged in this way will either end up fighting back, or refuse to see you any more. But take care! Don't use the method on people you don't know very well, or who you're dependent upon, like a superior at work. The results of your questioning may not be entirely to your advantage!

If you feel your efforts have failed, persevere even if you get the feeling you're banging your head against a wall. Don't become a defeatist too! You'll have to deal with the other person's frustration. If they've been a complainer for a long time, then you mustn't expect your rational suggestions to have an immediate effect. You may even provoke a whole new series of complaints, in which case you may get irritated and start to lose interest. Don't give up now! Take a few deep breaths, then interrupt the stream of complaints and start again. Sometimes just saying something like, 'All right, but let's get back to the question I asked earlier on . . .' may be enough to do the trick. Because, with chronic complainers, just like with surgical aggressive types (although for different reasons) it's futile to try to be tactful or polite. These people are too obsessed by their problems to get upset if you interrupt them or insist they be more specific. So don't hesitate to interrupt by raising your voice, or by using a gesture to get them to stop talking.

Your Training Programme

Dealing with complainers and other negative types, listening to them and helping them to take positive measures requires an unusual degree of objectivity and neutrality. After all, life throws so many problems our way, we don't have to make them the main subject of our conversation! Nevertheless, if you wish to assert yourself, both with others and for yourself, you have to learn to resolve this kind of problem. Your career may be at stake, or an important relationship, or simply your peace of mind – the rewards are well worth it.

Exercise: Rewrite Your Own History

Who has never suffered from injustice or been badly treated by others? We're all victims at some time or other, either during childhood or as adults. We probably don't think much about these incidents, which is why we don't become complainers. However, if you want to help others by using the rewriting history technique, you first have to be able to use it on yourself.

First, take a sheet of paper and write down circumstances when you felt like a victim. When your list is complete, answer these three questions:

- How did my behaviour contribute to making it happen?
- What did I do to encourage the situation? (Give precise facts.)
- How did I let it happen?

If you found a number of incidents where you felt like a victim, do the exercise for each one. You'll feel lighter, as if a burden has been lifted from your mind, and you'll experience a renewed sense of your own power.

Now, write a list of at least fifty things that you feel obligated to do, starting each sentence with '**I have to . . .**', for example, 'I have to declare my income . . .', 'I have to visit my wife's parents . . .', 'I have to mow the lawn . . .', and so on. When the list is complete, read it over and take time to become aware how you feel. Write down how you feel.

Now, take your fifty obligations and write them down again, only this time use the words '**I choose to . . .**' at the beginning of each sentence. So '*I choose to* declare my income . . .' '*I choose to* visit my wife's parents . . .' '*I choose to* mow the lawn . . .' Finished? Now how do you feel? Take a moment to add any positive things you choose to do that come to mind.

If you take the time to apply the 'I have to – I choose to' process described earlier for each obligation you may find the worst possible consequence of not acting is still preferable to doing action. In this case, you will know that you can choose not to do something. For example, you can choose not to water the lawn, in which case the grass will dry up and you won't have a lawn any more. If you don't care, then that's fine.

This exercise may help you to discover something about your real power over the world around you, and make you a freer person. You can then go on to share the experience with the complainers you meet and help them in turn to assume responsibility for their choices.

Exercise: Keep a Journal

As you saw in the previous chapter, it can be very useful to keep a journal of your encounters with difficult people, both complainers and other negative types. Use the following model.

Place and date:
Situation:
1. What the other person said:

2. What I replied:

3. What I should have replied:

4

Clam Types

Noticing his new neighbour is working in the garden, Jack remembers something he wanted to ask him. Walking over to the hedge, a smile on his face, Jack says hello and tries to start a discussion:

Jack: 'Your daughter and mine are in the same class . . .'
Neighbour: no reaction.
Jack: 'Helen told me she likes Claire a lot. Did Claire say anything to you?'
Neighbour: gives an indistinct grunt.
Jack: 'I thought that since the girls are becoming such good friends, we could work out some kind of arrangement for babysitting, if it's convenient, of course.'
Neighbour: 'Hmm . . .'
Jack: 'Well, if it doesn't work for you, we'll have to figure out something else . . .' Jack sighs and walks away.

―――――――

An economist presents a verbal summary of a report she has prepared for her superior, which he was supposed to have read beforehand. After stating her conclusions, she waits for her boss to comment:

Boss: 'Mmm . . .'
Economist: 'Is there something you don't understand? Maybe I should clarify some of the points . . .'
Boss: 'Mmm, no . . .'
Economist: 'Well, what do you think? Is it all right?'
Boss: 'Well . . . hmm . . .'
Economist: 'Sir! Will you please just tell me what you think?!'

f you're confronted with a clam, you'll be lucky to get a response more han two syllables long. Clams are probably the most exasperating of lifficult types. Just when you're expecting a clear response, or when you leed an explanation, or when you're hoping to start a conversation – hey close themselves off.

How can you differentiate between a clam and someone who just loesn't talk much? You have to be careful. Some people only speak vhen they have something interesting to say; they're incapable of small alk. Other people will wait until they have a coherent answer before replying. So what's the difference between clams and people who just don't talk much? Well, if you have ever had to deal with these two types, you will know it's almost impossible to mix them up. Let's look at the first example and imagine that Jack's neighbour isn't a clam, but just a person who doesn't talk much:

Jack: 'Your daughter and mine are in the same class . . .'
Neighbour: no discernible reaction.
Jack: Helen told me she likes Claire a lot. Did Claire say anything to you?'
Neighbour: 'No, she didn't say anything to me about it . . .'
Jack: 'I thought that since the girls are becoming such good friends . . .'
Neighbour: 'I'll talk to my wife about it, if you like.'

Do you see the difference? Laconic persons don't beat around the bush when asked to respond to a direct or indirect question. They simply keep quiet when they have nothing further to say.

The reasons why a person is unable to respond when you're trying to communicate are much more varied than for the other difficult types. There are a number of kinds of clams, all very different from each other. You should be very careful when interpreting their behaviour. In fact, the only way to get an accurate idea of what's going on is to make the clam talk, and then to listen very closely to what they say.

The Silence of Rejection

Becoming a wall of silence in order to express resentment is a weapon you may have used yourself – or you may have been its victim. To be the target of this type of behaviour can be one of the hardest situations to deal with in relations with difficult people. There are people whose resentment is so strong they remain stubbornly silent for extremely long periods, and resist all attempts at opening up to communication. Couples who have stopped talking to each other and who communicate only through written notes have been humorously portrayed in films and books. However, when it happens in real life – when parents stop talking to their children or to each other – the situation is serious.

You can understand a person being silent after a fight – but how can you explain it with someone you have no cause to disagree with? First of all, you may fall into a category which the clam rejects systematically. The simple fact of having differently shaped eyes, or talking with an accent, or just being perceived as an outsider or someone who is better off can be enough to trigger the clam reaction.

This is the worst kind of rejection to accept because it's so difficult to understand. Unless you have some inside information about the person who is rejecting you, you'll probably ask yourself, 'What is it about me this person can't accept?' or, 'What have I done?' Don't expect clams to explain their motives and feelings to you. To do so would be to recognize you as a separate and equal human being, which is exactly what they refuse to do.

Automatic Rejection Mechanism

The irrational and extremist aspects of this kind of rejection may lead you to think there's nothing you can do about this. However, that is not the case. A person who behaves in this way reduces you to one or two characteristics which serve to justify the rejection. They remain blind to everything else about you – especially your qualities. As long as they can maintain an image of you as a limited caricature, they can cut off all attempts at communication by clamming up. This is due to their automatic rejection mechanism, over which they have no control.

If you're dealing with someone whom you don't know, and who you probably won't see again, there's not much you can do to rectify the situation. But if you're going to be seeing the person on a regular basis, fortunately there's hope.

Above all, stay calm. If possible, maintain a benevolent attitude towards the person. To change the basis of the relationship, you have to give the person a chance to know you better, to discover your multiple dimensions. As soon as the clam starts to become aware of your other characteristics, it will be impossible to continue treating you in such a one-dimensional fashion – you will be perceived in a new light. It's highly probable they will then start behaving normally towards you.

It's due to this phenomenon that groups of human beings are capable of being deadly enemies under one set of conditions, but can live peacefully side by side under other conditions. Whenever hate rules the day, you can be sure to find mutual ignorance and a deformed view of reality as the underlying cause. When the communities live peacefully together, it's because they understand and appreciate each other.

The Silence of Protection

'Madeline, can you tell me who messed up the photocopy machine again? Whoever it was didn't use the right paper.'

'Uuh . . .'

'I won't let it go this time! You're not leaving here until you tell me who is responsible . . .'

Madeline's face turns to stone. No one is going to make her denounce her best friend. She resumes her work, making it clear she's not going to change her mind. Not knowing how to deal with the situation, her boss is forced to accept defeat.

When someone clams up in order to avoid conversation, it may be because they have something to hide, and wish at all cost to avoid a potentially painful confrontation. Refusing to answer a question, or answering only in monosyllables allows a person to avoid having to lie. It's unlikely you'll be able to get the person to change their mind. The problem is simply that they don't know how to lie. If Madeline had been able to smile sweetly and say, 'I don't have the slightest idea who broke the machine . . .', then the only thing you could do would be to believe her, or call her an outright liar, which is a serious accusation.

You're dealing with someone who can't lie because of their own ethical code, and who is prevented from betraying a friend for the same reason – you can imagine the inner conflict this causes! Their last resort is to remain silent. But, as we'll see later, even silence conveys a message, which you'll learn how to decipher so you can read clams like an open book.

The Silence of Suppression

Gilbert comes home and finds his wife upset. It isn't the first time, and he recognizes the signs immediately. Worried, he asks, 'Is anything wrong?', but this just irritates her more. 'No!' she snaps back. Of course, this solves nothing. Gilbert is sure something has happened, but his wife just goes about getting dinner ready, an absent look in her eyes.

Finally, Gilbert loses patience. He has to know what happened. 'Listen,' he says, his voice tense, 'something's bothering you. You're not yourself. Tell me what happened!' 'Nothing, nothing at all!' replies his wife. The more she refuses to talk, the more certain Gilbert is that something is really wrong.

Later on in the evening, he asks her again. She suddenly bursts out crying, 'Monica has breast cancer!' Despite the bad news, Gilbert feels much better – there's nothing worse than being kept in the dark.

More often than we are aware, people suppress emotional crises by hiding behind silence. They grit their teeth and refuse to let others know about their pain, fearing that if they let themselves go, even for a moment, they'll be swept away in a tide of emotion. But if an emotion isn't expressed, it stagnates, pent up in the body where it does its nasty work by tensing muscles, causing cramps, skin rashes, ulcers and the like. As time passes, all conscious recollection of the initial emotion may disappear – but the body never forgets. It's much better to express emotion.

The way you can help clams is by giving them an opportunity to open up, instead of remaining blocked, teeth clenched. Your efforts to get a clam to talk may result in the person bursting into tears or anger. If you're not prepared, you may be somewhat frightened by this response. However, remember you are not the cause of the person's suffering – all you did was to open a door. All you need to do next is remain quietly by the person's side, ready to offer assistance. If they are in pain, just pass the tissues, and if the person is a friend, maybe offer a hug or a pat on the back.

Provoking such outpourings in the work place would of course be embarrassing. However, you can't expect colleagues to be completely free of emotion, so try to discern any hidden motives which may lie behind their refusal to communicate; try to find out what the *real* problem is. If you feel the person is too charged up emotionally, stop, and suggest they see their doctor, or take a few days off: *your role is not to provide emotional therapy . . .*

The Silence of Boredom

Have you ever been to a social gathering where you know absolutely no one, have nothing in common with anyone, and remain silent the entire evening because you can't find anything to say? This is the most common motive behind the silence of clam types. These people live on another planet – they don't understand you, and don't know how to communicate with you. Because of this they may find your company boring, but this isn't always the case.

I once had a passionate affair with a beautiful young woman, with whom there was an immediate mutual attraction. When we held hands, a powerful current flowed between us – but aside from that, she was completely silent. None of the topics of conversation I brought up could get her to say one word. She listened to me intently, but whenever I stopped talking there was dead silence. Although she was really in love with me, and proved it by crossing an entire continent just to be with me, I'd hoped she'd stay where I left her, because the idea of living through more of those painful silences gave me the shivers. A relationship is not based solely on physical attraction, and with this woman I experienced the boredom of love. At the time, I had no idea why such a barrier existed between us, despite our physical affinity, although my research in later years helped me to find the answer.

Do You Speak the Same Language?

You may think that all you have to do to communicate with someone is to speak the same language. I speak English, you speak English, so we can communicate, right? Wrong:

Martine: 'I'm listening to you, but I don't know what you're talking about. It really makes no sense to me.'

Mark: 'Can't you see what I'm doing?! I'm trying to use a little imagination to get you to understand what I mean!'
Violet: 'I really don't feel you're making sense. Your images just leave me cold.'

Do you think these three people have a chance of understanding each other? Maybe, but to do so they'll have to make a concerted effort to *translate* what they're saying. Martine uses a predominantly auditory language, while Mark's is visual. Violet, on the other hand, uses words that refer to her feelings only.

These three ways of perceiving the world are related to our three principle senses: hearing, seeing, and touching. How can these people use their senses so differently? Psychologists have learned that we select information perceived through our five senses. Sometimes we're all ears, at other times we depend solely on our vision, and at others we're sensitive to touch. We can also be overwhelmed by a scent, or by the taste of food. You'll notice, for example, that it's very difficult to be fully attentive to what is being said around you while concentrating on a delicious taste – it is impossible to be fully aware of the perceptions of all five senses at the same time.

We are constantly selecting and concentrating on a single aspect of our experience. This selection process begins at a very early age. Every one of us was conditioned to place more emphasis on one of our perceptions. By the time we reach adulthood, we are firmly placed in one of three groups: hearers, visualizers, or feelers. Because of this we develop preferences for the visual arts; or the quality of a person's voice, or by touch.

Is this sufficient to explain why some people shut themselves off from you? Let's look at the case of my silent lover. Although we could communicate through touching in a fairly intense manner, we lived in two separate universes. While she was a visual person, content with what her eyes perceived, I place a lot of emphasis on the sound of someone's voice. But that wasn't the only reason for her silence; there were other differences that made our reaching a common understanding highly improbable.

The Principles of Affinity

Having an affinity for someone means feeling close to them naturally, without effort. Instant sympathy could be another term for it, although affinities don't always appear the first time you meet someone; you may have to get to know a person better first. The opposite of affinity is the feeling of having nothing in common with a person. The result of such a relationship is boredom, indifference, and sometimes even hate. A great deal of clam behaviour stems from this.

Six Ways of Sorting Information

In addition to developing one sensory function, we are also equipped with filters that sort out the information we receive from the exterior world – certain things attract our attention, others we ignore completely. Our brains couldn't cope if we remained open to all incoming information, at all times, with the same level of intensity. The disadvantage of this process is that we get only a partial and incomplete view of the world, and this leads to disagreements with people who have developed different sets of filters from our own. That's why we tend to favour people who use the same filters as we do. When we perceive reality in the same way as someone else, we feel an immediate affinity for that person. When we don't use the same filters, we feel a gulf separating us, and we may wonder what we can do to cross over.

Among all the ways we differ from each other, one is of particular interest to us. Think of the best holiday you can remember taking, or one that you would like to take. Depending on the category, or 'tribe' you belong to, you may recall vividly coloured and varied images, or things you heard and said, or you'll remember tactile sensations (heat, comfort, etc.) and emotions. Set these aside, and what do you think of? Places? Activities? People? Events? Information? Objects? These are the six main categories which you, I, and everyone else use to sort information. We're not interested in all dimensions of an event, and there are even some we systematically ignore.

Let's look at the example of the dream vacation. Say you find yourself in a travel agency, and the agent is trying to sell you a cruise to Greece. He or she won't succeed by telling you about the marvellous locations to be found in Greece if what you're interested in are the people. Your decision will be based on whether your friend George is willing to accompany you, and on the kind of people you'll meet on the tour, and on whether or not the Greek natives have a reputation for being friendly to tourists. Neither will the agent succeed by telling you that the cruise is a unique event, if what you're interested in is action. You'll want to know about the activities available during the voyage. Diving? Windsurfing? And so on. As a last resort, the travel agent starts giving you all the information about the cruise – schedules, ports of call, distances you'll be travelling, exchange rates, average temperatures etc. Pretty soon you stop listening – your mind is elsewhere, and you respond to the agent's questions in monosyllables. What you're interested in are things. Is there anything interesting to buy in Greece? That's what you want to know.

Talkative one Day, Silent the Next

You can begin to understand why people stubbornly refuse to say a word, closing themselves off like a clam in its shell. A person may prattle on endlessly about their preferred activity, but have absolutely no interest in discussing something else. In the same way, it's not surprising that professions correspond to different filters: a landscape architect prefers locations; a psychologist or teacher prefers people; a researcher, information; an antique dealer, objects; a journalist, events; a sports professional, action, and so on.

The more we learn about human nature, the more we understand behaviour that may have seemed strange, and the more we can accept the differences between ourselves and others. In fact, by discovering which senses and which filters you use the least, and by using them more, you will increase your ability to perceive through all five senses, vastly increasing your sensitivity in all directions. This in turn will enable you to reach out to people who previously seemed inaccessible. By speaking the same language and adjusting your point of view to suit their affinities, you will be able to help those people who have been locked in silence to open up and communicate.

Dealing with Clam Types

First of all, stay calm. You may be tempted to interpret a person's silence as rejection, or to give in to a desire to shake the person up in order to get some kind of reaction. Don't! There's nothing worse than saying or doing something that denigrates the person. Don't think that a remark like, 'I get the feeling there's a sponge in your head instead of a brain!' will get them to start talking. On the contrary, this kind of remark will only fuel the clam's resolve to remain silent. Instead, if you let the person know you're sincerely interested in listening, you'll get what you want a lot more easily.

Now you have to study and practise the methods for overcoming silence. Don't try to read between the lines; get the person to talk. This avoids increased tension for yourself, and helps the other person.

Ask the Right Questions

You ask a colleague to join you in your office to discuss certain aspects of your work together. You know that despite being very competent, they have always been closed with you in the past. However, you'd like to get them to talk to you, because you're pretty sure they have some interesting ideas to offer. To do this, you can ask some questions – but not just any questions.

You're not going to get anywhere in your attempts to help someone to open up to you by asking closed questions, which are questions which can easily be answered by a simple yes or no. For example, avoid questions like, 'Do you agree?' or 'Would you choose A or B?' Such dead-end questions allow the clam to remain as shut off as ever.

Next, be careful you don't insinuate anything negative about the other person when asking a question. For example, if you say, 'Did you understand my question?' you're insinuating that they aren't answering because they are stupid. As we've seen, this is an excellent way *not* to get what you want. On the other hand, making positive insinuations in the questions you ask is a good way to make a person comfortable. For example, you could say, jokingly, 'Do I understand from your silence that you don't wish to share your expertise with me?' Even in this slightly provocative way, you're telling the person you value their opinion.

Don't Let Silence Embarrass You

Accompany your question with a sincerely inquisitive, but always polite, glance, and maintain this expression after you've finished asking the question. Don't worry about the silence that may follow. Clams sometimes have trouble formulating their ideas rapidly since they're not used to being called upon to do so. They may need a few moments to collect their thoughts. Just let your expression do the talking, and wait patiently for a response.

Like other difficult types, clams have formed habitual ways of reacting to situations which is in accord with their motive – to remain silent. They develop scenarios which they use, sometimes unknowingly, to get themselves off the hook without revealing anything. That's why they're thrown off balance if you react in an unexpected way; they momentarily lose their apparent shell of assurance. You can use this opening to ask the right kinds of questions.

Still, there aren't many people who are comfortable when silences occur during a conversation or a meeting. Clam types constantly make use of this phenomenon – they know, consciously or not, that every time they remain silent, someone will volunteer to fill the gap. Don't fall into the trap by getting upset, clearing your throat, sighing, or making small talk just to fill in the silent spaces. What should you do? Repeat your open-ended question every twenty seconds, maintaining the same cordial, inquisitive expression. If you feel guilty about forcing someone to speak against their will, then ask whether it's better just to let a clam continue hiding.

Even the most hardened clam types will eventually understand that you're not reacting the way everybody else has in the past, and that they won't be able to manipulate you. You probably won't have to ask the question more than two or three times.

However, if you find the 'interrogation' technique too aggressive, there's another fantastic method for helping people to talk: the 'suppose we . . .' technique. Here are a few examples:

You: 'Gerry, where do you think you're going to spend your holiday?'
Gerry: remains silent, meaning either, 'I don't know . . .', or 'I haven't decided yet . . .'

You: 'Suppose you'd already decided. Where would it be?'
Gerry: 'Oh, well, supposing I've made a decision, it could be a couple of weeks in the Caribbean, or maybe a week with my family in Italy.'

You: 'Monica, what's your opinion of the way our early retirement programme is working?'
Monica: remains silent, meaning she doesn't want to say anything before consulting her superiors.
You: 'Suppose it was your decision – what would you do?'
Monica: 'Well, if it were my decision, the first thing I'd do would be to . . .'

And there you are – with all the information you need!

If Nothing Works . . .

You've equipped yourself with a battery of techniques for helping even the most hardened clam types. But perhaps all your efforts have failed. No doubt you still haven't been able to understand how these people perceive the world differently from you, and adapt your approach to their outlook accordingly. Discerning these differences requires concentration and patient training.

There may be something else you need to correct. The best way to help someone to open up is to show you have a real interest in them. Very often our interest is just a façade. We ask questions without being really interested in the answers. We're more inclined to want to talk about ourselves, and attract attention to ourselves. Clams can invariably detect this. They are usually very sensitive people, who protect themselves by hiding behind a shell. They will know for certain whether your interest is real or feigned. If it isn't real, any technique you use will be a poor substitute.

Telephone Clams

There are people who, although capable of engaging in normal conversation most of the time, find themselves speechless when forced to talk on the telephone, even to people they know well. When we converse – or attempt to converse – with these occasional clams, we get the impression we're engaged in a monologue rather than a dialogue. At least with the person in front of us we can tell from their expression and body language that what we're saying is being registered. But on the phone, we can't even be sure of that.

In the great majority of cases, telephone clams are people who lack self-confidence, who are timid and introverted, who have to make a great effort to assert themselves, and to acquire a minimum of self-assurance. Although they give the impression of not having a communication problem, as soon as they are holding a telephone receiver, they seem to be overcome by the shyness they've taken such pains to hide. That's why shy people, although they may have learned to assert themselves with others, need the constant reassurance of their listeners in the form of subtle body language and approving gestures to maintain their confidence. The telephone eliminates all these subtle forms of communication. The clam can't see the person on the other end of the line, which provokes silence.

What Can You Do?

The first part of your strategy remains the same – ask questions which can't be answered in monosyllables. Since you can't accompany the question with an interested and inquisitive look, try to express your interest in the tone of your voice by making it more expressive than in a face-to-face conversation. You can also accompany your question with statements such as: 'I'd really like to hear your opinion on this subject . . .', or 'I place a lot of value on your opinion . . .', or 'I'm counting on your comments . . .' and so on. Once you've asked the question, give the person time to organize their thoughts, and then ask again if no answer is forthcoming.

If the person on the other end remains silent, avoid getting upset at all cost. Don't make any aggressive remarks. If you do, you may turn the person into a permanent clam, instead of an occasional one. This doesn't mean you should let the person hang up without getting what you want. Make it clear that you intend to call back after allowing the person time to organize their thoughts. Set up an appointment for a follow-up call, and as a last resort, suggest meeting the person face to face. Personal encounters will make communicating a lot easier for both of you!

Your Training Programme

Reading advice on how to communicate with clam types isn't enough; to learn how to deal with them requires practice.

Discerning Sensory Input

It's important to know what your own predominating sense is: visual, auditory, or tactile. (We're leaving out the olfactory and taste senses because they rarely predominate in humans.) Then, once you've detected a person's predominant sense, you simply have to make an effort to speak the same language as they do. Easier said than done, you may be thinking – and you're right. Difficult to do, but by no means impossible, and well worth the effort, since accomplishing this will make you an excellent and effective communicator.

What Problems are Involved?

There are two main problems you will encounter: learning to recognize a person's predominant sense, and learning to express yourself using language different from your own. At the end of this book, you'll find two self-diagnostic tests (Appendix 2). The first – called Visual–Auditory–Sensory Test (VAS) – will help you to determine your predominant sense. Respond as spontaneously as possible. The aim of the test is above all to make you more aware of the dimensions of your personality, not to define it conclusively. To get an idea of the predominant senses in others, make photocopies of the test and ask friends and colleagues to complete it. They'll acquire a better under-standing of themselves, and you'll understand why communicating with them may sometimes have been difficult in the past. The second test will help you to determine the main criteria you use to sort information.

If you could ask a clam type to complete the two tests; doing the exercises together would be a large step forward in improving your communication. Of course, you can't take the tests with you wherever you go, and fortunately, there are other ways to determine people's predominant senses.

Which Words, and Why?

The words we use are often a direct reflection of our predominant sense. When I say something like, 'This sounds like a conversation between deaf mutes . . .', what sense am I evoking? Hearing, of course. The fact that I use this expression is not due to chance – it shows that hearing is my predominant sense. I could have said something like, 'They need someone to spell it out for them . . .' (visual), or 'You can cut the tension between them with a knife . . .' (tactile).

To help you to determine a person's predominant sense, below is a list of words and expressions which generally characterize each sense.

Characteristic Words

Visual	Auditory	Tactile	Non-specific
perspective –	I hear what	have a feeling –	attitude –
point of view –	you're saying –	premonition –	consider –
watch over –	listen to this –	vibrate –	persevere –
keep an eye on	rings a bell – let	insensitive –	perception –
– my mind's a	me explain –	heavy – gloomy	reveal – emit –
blank – look	strike a chord –	– striking – put	absent – simple
this over –	speechless –	my finger on it	– ostentatious –
point out –	silence –	– seize control –	attentive –
illustrate –	harmonious –	put the pressure	ignore – expose
looks familiar –	I'm listening –	on – tighten the	– note – go
take another	help me to	screws – warm/	beyond –

look – enlighten	understand – I	cold	identify –
– blinded –	forgot to	atmosphere –	conceive –
symmetry –	mention – refer	soft-rough – gut	repeat –
brilliant – I	to – fall on deaf	feeling – get	remember . . .
don't see it that	ears . . .	things moving –	
way . . .		sad – in	
		depth . . .	

Analyzing a Conversation

You now have the information to determine through words and expressions the predominant sensory input of a person. The best way to practise this technique is to note down key words while listening to someone speak. As you won't be able to do this while engaged in a conversation, you can use television interviews, or conversations you overhear, or ask friends or relatives to tell you about trips they took and so on. Note down the key words and expressions the person uses, for example:

> . . . trip to Brittany . . . wind whistling . . . height of the cliffs . . . tremendous silence at night . . . chanting in the churches . . . whisper of the ocean . . . I said to myself . . .

Clearly, we're dealing with an auditory person. You don't have to fill pages and pages with your notes; sometimes all you need are two or three sentences.

If a person uses a lot of non-specific expressions, or a mixture of visual, auditory, and tactile terms, you may not be sure which sense is dominant. In such cases you will have to be patient, and analyze the language more carefully.

Exercise: From One Language to Another

A good way to practise a language that isn't your own is to use a simple story like 'Little Red Riding Hood' and repeat it out loud, concentrating on one set of sensory inputs each time:

Visual: Once there was a little girl with golden blonde hair and rosy cheeks, wearing a grey skirt, and a blouse with little white and blue checks . . .

Auditory: She heard her mother's voice calling her from the kitchen. Her mother's footsteps pounded in the hallway, and then she burst into the room shouting, 'Do you have to be so noisy, Little Red?!'

Tactile: Little Red grabbed her basket and sighed. She tested the cake her mother had given her – it felt a little warm. The idea of taking a walk through the forest made her feel happy with expectation.

Just continue the story in the same way. I don't know a better way to practise using the different sensory aspects of language.

Categories of Information Sorting

Human beings see reality in different ways, emphasizing one aspect over others. To find out what category you fall into, complete the tests in Appendix 2. No reflection or calculation is required – just answer the questions as spontaneously as possible. You'll probably be surprised by how accurate the results are. Make copies of the test, and distribute them to friends, colleagues, and family – and especially to any clam types you know.

If You Can't Use the Test . . .

To find out what a person's principal information-sorting criteria is, you have to listen attentively to what they say – the filter they use will quickly become apparent. Certain persons only talk about others. Some concentrate on places, others provide very precise information. The same method used for determining a predominant sense is also used here – just note down key words and expressions.

Asking someone to tell you about one of the most beautiful days in their life is a good way to find out what the person's information-sorting filter is. Was it when they got a new car (object)? Or was it a party with good friends (people)? Was it related to a particularly beautiful sunset in some exotic place (location)? Does the person provide a lot of detailed information?

Few people use only one information-sorting filter – they usually appear in pairs. Some criteria will be totally ignored, and that's where problems can arise. Imagine that objects are extremely important to you, while your spouse places hardly any importance on objects at all. This could lead to serious misunderstandings!

Exercise: Adapting to Different Criteria

This exercise consists of thinking of ways to present a project to someone by appealing to each of the six filters.

To sell the idea of a trip to Greece what would you say to someone whose emphasis is on:

- events

- locations

- actions

- people

- information

- objects

Some categories could prove very troublesome, especially those you don't relate to at all. Other people will be only too happy to show you how to speak their language – and they may also want to make the effort to learn yours!

5

The Dangers of
Playing Games

John and Susan have been married for ten years. John is a manager in a private company, Susan is a nurse, working for a fairly low salary. A year ago, the couple agreed to cut their family spending so John could take off one day a week and go back to school.

Their marriage anniversary is coming up. In the past they'd celebrated in a good restaurant, but this year Susan decides to surprise John with a meal at home. She starts looking through recipe books for something sumptuous, but inexpensive. She has bought some material to make a new bathrobe for her husband, and has bought some perfumed candles to help make the evening a special occasion.

The day of their anniversary arrives. Feeling proud of her work, Susan barely gets everything finished before John comes home from work. Finally he comes in, all excited, saying, 'Susan! Tonight we're going out! I made reservations at a new restaurant. The hell with our budget! We're going to live it up!'

'Wait a minute', Susan says, and leads him to the dining-room lit with candles, a bottle of champagne cooled and ready to open. 'I thought we could eat at home tonight.' Reluctantly, John agrees to eat at home, knowing he has another surprise.

After the meal, John takes a little box wrapped in gold paper out of his pocket and gives it to Susan, who feels a little uneasy as she tears off the wrapping. Inside is a superb gold bracelet set with sapphires, exactly like the one she had admired in a shop window a few weeks past. Tears well up in her eyes. John, thinking it's because she's so happy, and feeling very pleased with himself, tries to take her in his arms. But Susan pushes him away, and throws the bracelet to the ground.

'How could you!' she cries. 'When I look at that bracelet, all it makes me think of are the hundred-and-one things I have to do to save money every week! And you think you can have fun playing the prince and buying expensive toys because it amuses you, even if it puts us into debt for the next five years!'

John is speechless. He tries to explain that he is just trying to show his gratitude for all the sacrifices Susan's been making so he can get the qualifications he needs for a promotion. He gets caught up in defending his actions, which leads to a long, drawn-out quarrel where both sides blame each other for all the little grievances they've been hoarding up over their years of living together.

This is called verbal ping-pong: a dangerous little drama where both sides hurl hostile messages at each other which are often contradictory and always indirect. Old wounds are opened, and new ones are created. Here's another example:

> Mark is nineteen years old. He lives with his mother, Joanne, and his two younger brothers, aged eight and twelve. Joanne has a full-time job, and also takes care of the housework. According to her, 'Mark is a very good boy. But I must have told him a hundred times to wipe his feet before coming into the kitchen; he's always leaving his muddy tracks on the floor.'

Why?

> Joanne is very busy. She can't afford to pay a babysitter when she goes out, so Mark is regularly left in charge.
>
> Mark think she goes out too much, but Joanne is well aware of the dangers of being a single mother, cut off from all social activities, so she makes an effort not to lose touch with her friends. When Mark objects, she tells him that, in her opinion, if he doesn't help her out, it's because he doesn't love her.
>
> How does Mark rebel against her accusation? He tracks mud across the kitchen floor. Then he apologizes, gives his mother a hug, and tells her what a good cook she is! This show of affection prevents Joanne from venting her anger, so she must (unconsciously) look for another way to get revenge. When someone invites her over for dinner the following Saturday she accepts immediately, explaining that Mark will be able to stay home and babysit. She conveniently 'forgets' that Mark has been invited to a party on Saturday, even though he made sure to tell her, and put it on the kitchen calendar.

Because they are incapable of saying out loud what they're thinking, Mark and Joanne have embarked on a dangerous ride which may lead to a real confrontation, and possibly rupture their relationship, despite the affection they feel for each other. Deep down, each blames the other for being difficult, but neither mother nor son dares, or knows how to, cross over the barrier growing between them.

Why Play Games?

We've all played such games at one time or another with someone dear to us. And that is one of the characteristics of this kind of emotional duelling: it's always played between people who are close to each other, and it begins very early on in a relationship. In fact, children are masters at this game, which often results in a kind of emotional blackmail. Let's listen to what a woman, divorced and living alone with her six-year-old daughter, has to say about a dinner invitation she extended to a man she is thinking about marrying:

> 'I put Tina to bed at eight o'clock, and asked her to behave herself while Dennis was here. She didn't misbehave or start crying – that would have been easy! What she did, was to call me to her room every five minutes. Either she was thirsty, or she couldn't find her teddy bear, or she wanted me to kiss her goodnight . . . She drove me crazy! It's lucky Dennis likes kids!'

What made Tina act this way? Her fear of being rejected. This feeling, although obvious (as a child Tina was not as adept at hiding her feelings as adults are) was the motivating force behind her contradictory messages. Her behaviour was a natural reaction to the threat she felt was being directed at her relationship with her mother.

Adults who do not wish to break off a relationship but who at the same time want to change something about it send even more indirect messages, hoping to avoid a direct confrontation. This is the case, for example, with couples who criticize each other in public because they're afraid to do so when they're alone. Let's take another look at our examples . . .

Mark thinks his mother takes advantage of him, but he doesn't dare come right out and say it because he's afraid of being accused of selfishness and of not loving her. So he makes an indirect (unconscious) statement of protest by muddying the kitchen floor, and then disguises this hostile message in a show of affection.

Joanne is afraid of getting angry with her son, thereby losing his precious help, and so tries to avoid a confrontation as well. She prefers hearing an outwardly positive message (Mark's apologies, hugs, and compliments), and agrees to ignore the negative message (mud on the kitchen floor).

In John and Susan's case, Susan thinks that:

- all her sacrifices and efforts to manage the household on a reduced budget were not important;
- her husband doesn't care, or takes her efforts for granted – they're nothing to be proud of;

- her husband's manly pride and his need to be the breadwinner in the family made him go out and splurge on a luxurious gift they couldn't afford, with no thought of tomorrow.

As for John, frustrated in his role of benefactor, he pretends to see Susan as an ungrateful wife, embittered by the financial sacrifices she's had to make over the last year, and ultimately unworthy of the magnificent present he bought her.

John and Susan are not on the same wavelength; their line of communication has been broken. But, fearing to destroy the relationship completely, neither is capable of saying openly what they think about their respective attitudes.

What Are the Results?

It's often tempting to adopt the philosophy of 'an eye for an eye'. When verbal ping-pong has become the normal mode of communication in a relationship, however, both parties become victims of each other's hostility. Unfortunately, the end result is often precisely what both sides are trying to avoid: the end of the relationship. The only alternative is for both sides to accept verbal ping-pong as a normal way of life, and remain together while continually accusing each other of being difficult people. Both sides say and do terrible things to each other, which they then try to patch up with shows of affection. Being together becomes mutually aggravating, and finally intolerable. Any compromise or negotiation becomes impossible, and the relationship eventually breaks apart.

Even if the situation doesn't deteriorate completely, the relationship suffers. Sometimes couples get into the habit of avoiding any subject that might cause friction, afraid of mutual rejection and the end of the relationship. They assume that because one aspect of their behaviour is being criticized or rejected, the rest will be as well. This is exactly the way a child thinks: *any* kind of refusal by the parents is felt to be *total* rejection. Under such conditions, how can a relationship be expected to evolve, develop, and mature?

What are the Remedies?

Are you involved in a similar situation? Do you consider someone close to you to be difficult while knowing they think the same of you? Do something about it before it's too late. Not only will you save a relationship that's important to you, you'll also find that making an effort is a perfect way of developing character and self-esteem.

Both your attitudes stem from a desire for change that neither one of you is able to express openly, because you both fear that doing so will result in total rejection. No matter which of you is the dominating force in the relationship, you both feel powerless to effect a change.

Let's take another look at one of our examples. Although Joanne is Mark's mother ad ostensibly the head of the family, she is afraid of the way in which her son will react if she forces him to wipe his feet before entering the kitchen; she's afraid to lose his help in caring for the other children, which she desperately needs. In this kind of difficult relationship, neither side takes the initiative and makes the desired changes. Here are some steps to follow to remedy this, or a similar, situation.

Become aware of the problem. First, you have to determine the circumstances in which you're likely to develop a game of verbal ping-pong. But be careful! Don't fall into the trap of trying to read the other person's mind – you must first become aware of *your* problems. It's hard enough dealing with your own mind!

The following exercise, which may be aptly called an examination of the unconscious, will help you to discover what is bothering you, why you tend to react in a certain way, and what circumstances seem to provoke this type of negative reaction.

Exercise: Examining Your Unconscious

First, get comfortable, with a pen and paper handy. Then:

- Try to recall at least two recent arguments you had with the person in question. Remember the exact circumstances.
- Try to analyze your feelings at those moments. Be honest with yourself; hide absolutely nothing.
- Write down everything you felt, openly and frankly.

It's important you use the first person – I – when making your notes, in order to emphasize the fact that you're talking about yourself. Write only precise facts and your feelings: 'Yesterday I felt ripped-off and betrayed when Sally accused me of being dishonest . . .' This process of analysis will help you to see yourself more clearly. In addition, writing your feelings on paper will help you to gain some objectivity towards what happened, and will take the drama out of the confrontation.

Don't allow a relationship to deteriorate. As soon as you feel a relationship is starting to turn sour, and realize the other person is saying or doing things that upset you, *don't wait – attack the problem immediately!* You may be thinking it's impossible to do something every time someone says or does something unpleasant. How do you know when it's the right time to express your negative feelings?

In a relationship that isn't working, both sides accumulate negative 'points'. At first, they don't amount to much, and you probably let them pass without reacting. But the event sticks in your memory, whether you like it or not. Then another incident occurs. Again you decide it isn't serious enough for an out-and-out confrontation, and let it pass. A second negative 'point' is added to the first. As time passes, more incidents occur, some more serious than others. Each one adds to your collection of points. And then one day, something happens. It may be a minor incident – not half as serious as some of the things that have already happened – but for you it's the last straw, and you blow your top.

This process is well known to anyone who has lived through a relationship. It also has been studied by psychologists, who have devised a rule which advises people to *never go to sleep bearing a grudge towards someone*. A variation of this rule is never let more than six hours pass before addressing your resentment towards someone. In other words, never let a problem grow to the point that it infects the relationship. The hostile messages directed at you by the other person are really calls for help; don't respond by being aggressive and perpetuating the vicious circle. The following example, unfortunately, concerns a situation which is still quite common among couples:

When Marilyn and Jack had their first child two years ago, Marilyn gave up her job as a clothes designer. It was a job she liked, but Jack, as well as all her inlaws, insisted she stop working and stay home to care for the baby. Marilyn was afraid to refuse – to do so would have made her appear callous, unworthy to be a mother, and ungrateful to Jack. She pushed away feelings of disappointment, and her growing lack of self-esteem.

Jack comes home every night full of stories about what happened that day at work. Because Marilyn is afraid to complain that taking care of the baby full-time bores her, and that she misses her work, she seeks ways unconsciously and indirectly to vent her unhappiness. For example, she forgets to call the plumber to fix a leak; she loses the car keys; she accepts invitations to events she knows her husband won't enjoy, and so on. In other words, Marilyn is unconsciously looking for ways to annoy Jack, without actually provoking a direct confrontation.

Jack admires Marilyn's many qualities, but considers her a little difficult to handle at times; but since he's so comfortable in the current arrangement, he doesn't want to ask any direct questions that may upset the *status quo*. Deep down he knows Marilyn is unhappy, that she feels confined and unappreciated. But he doesn't want to be the one to raise the issue by asking questions.

How can Marilyn and Jack solve their problem? Simple as it seems, all they need to do is sit down and have a frank discussion. They should first analyze their personal problems separately, and then negotiate with each other. Because both of them are afraid to jeopardize the relationship, Jack responds to Marilyn's behavioural quirks with irritated indulgence, and Marilyn responds to Jack's male 'superiority' with seemingly insignificant, yet repeated acts of petty revenge. They are both slowly poisoning each other's existence – and the relationship. Don't follow their example!

Share your feelings. How you can be sure that negative points are accumulating in a relationship? It's very simple: when you're communicating positively with someone, you are left feeling content, energized, serene. These are signs that the relationship is working well. When communication is negative, you are left feeling heavy and empty. These are danger signs, and you should act immediately to restore harmony and balance.

I remember an incident that happened to me, shortly after I studied the principles I'm explaining to you now. One of my best friends phoned me to tell me that he urgently needed to borrow a large sum of money. I happened to have just enough money in my deposit account at the time, which I didn't need to use right away. However, I knew I'd be needing the money in a month, and that if I didn't have it back by then I'd be in serious trouble. So I offered to lend my friend the money, on condition he pay me back by the end of the month. He agreed, promising he would do so.

When I put the phone down, I felt overcome with anxiety. I knew my friend had been having money problems for a while, and that it was highly unlikely he would be able to pay me back on time. In the name of friendship I'd agreed to something I didn't feel comfortable with. There I was, pensive, worried, thinking about all the problems this would cause. I had to do something to rectify the situation.

I thought about my friend and his money problems. My offer of help had probably taken a great weight off his mind. How could I tell him I'd changed my mind, without losing his friendship? Here's where the golden rule applies: never let more than six hours pass . . . If I was going to lose a friend, I'd rather it was because I didn't lend him the money than because he couldn't pay it back! I called him back and explained why I felt uneasy about my decision. I talked about my problems, and the fact that I didn't want it to destroy our friendship, and that it was for that reason that I wasn't going to lend him the money.

We've remained the best of friends. He valued our friendship as much as I did, and didn't want to destroy it either. He appreciated my frankness, which was further proof of my affection for him. He didn't want to create problems for me, so he went and found someone else to borrow the money from who wasn't under the same pressure as I was.

Showing Your Vulnerability

Try your hand at being frank and open the next time an occasion arises. If you're unable to be open with someone, it's because you're afraid of being rejected. You fear losing the love of a person who is close to you if you don't play the role you believe is expected of you – a kind, generous, understanding person – even though you may find this confining and feel terribly exploited.

What would happen if you revealed what you're really thinking? If you let the person know you aren't really as generous, patient, kind, and understanding as you've made out to be? In its absolute sense, perfection is inhuman, and those who pretend to be perfect or demand perfection from others – the two often go hand in hand – are very difficult to take. They are a perpetual threat of our being found lacking, and of being rejected because of our inability to live up to their expectations. We have to recognize the value of our own, and other people's imperfections – the faults and weaknesses that make us human. Being vulnerable and imperfect brings us closer to other people, since it allows them to lower their own masks and reveal themselves as they really are.

Being close to someone only becomes possible when you accept your vulnerability instead of trying to hide it. Only then can a joyous exchange between two people occur – when you no longer have to hide your real self, and your needs. This is the paradox of being vulnerable: the more we believe we are weak and worthless, the more we need to hide our 'faults', and project an artificial image, convinced this is the only way to gain the confidence and respect of others. The more confident we are of our own worth, the more able we are to recognize our faults and imperfections, and the less we need to hide them. We know that nothing can cause us to lose the affection of those who really love us.

You have everything to gain by revealing your vulnerability to others, and letting them know that you fear being rejected by them, and esteem their respect and affection. Doing so will certainly improve the stability of your relationships.

Overcoming Resentment

During verbal ping-pong, all kinds of things come to the surface that have been accumulating over time. Each reproach stems from some kind of frustration, some incident which has been suppressed into a bitter memory. This accumulation of frustration builds into a tremendous amount of resentment, which finally explodes. This explosion only serves to feed our feelings of hate and resentment, creating a vicious circle which, fortunately, it's possible to break.

The Anatomy of Resentment

Resentment isn't hard to understand: it is produced every time an action does not correspond to an expectation. For example, say your child is rude to you. Well, you wouldn't want your child to be totally docile and nice all the time either. If you were able to accept the child's behaviour as being normal, or if you could love them despite this, their behaviour would produce absolutely no feelings of animosity or resentment in you. This doesn't mean you have to like it. But you can tolerate it, like you tolerate the cold weather in winter, or flu. You wouldn't accumulate resentment against flu, would you?

Resentment, on the other hand, arises because you have expectations. For example, when I work with a group of people, I'm sometimes a little impatient. Some people find this stimulating, and even thank me for it; others complain because they think I should be gentle and patient all the time. We have an image of the way we think other people should behave, in the same way they have an image of us. The problem is knowing to what point we should try to conform to other people's expectations.

One thing is certain: we are never obliged to fulfil other people's expectations. We have our own expectations, and so do they. What is essential to a healthy relationship is being able *to communicate our expectations*, so both sides know what they're up against. Then everything becomes a question of negotiation: I'll make an effort if you will too – then we can both be winners in this relationship.

Who Does Your Resentment Hurt?

You've allowed a lot of negative points to accumulate in your relations with certain people. You've patiently catalogued your frustrations, and these have gradually formed into a compact little ball of heavy, bitter, ugly matter that you carry with you permanently. This ball of poison is your resentment.

It's time to become aware that *you* are the one your resentment is hurting the most. The person you feel resentment against may not even know about it! This means you are twice a loser: first because of the initial frustration or disappointment you felt; and second because you have to carry these negative feelings around and suffer all the associated consequences. Yet there are people who would rather die than to give up their resentment. Hatred is even transmitted from one generation to another, so in time people find they know who to hate, even though they've forgotten why.

Ben's boss is a tyrant who runs his department like a slave driver, dominating and sometimes hurting his colleagues without even being aware of what he's doing – a real steamroller type. Even thinking about his boss sets Ben's little ball of resentment throbbing. He really hates his boss, and he's not the only one at the office who does. But this hatred is poisoning Ben's life. He has to make an effort to go to work every morning, and every time his boss asks him to do something, he grumbles and reluctantly obeys.

Ben has been in a bad mood since his new boss was appointed, and the repercussions are starting to show in his personal life. He loses patience with his wife and children a lot more easily, and the atmosphere when he's around is always heavy and tense. He's even finding it difficult to sleep, obsessed as he is with finding ways to vent his resentment, although he never actually does anything about it. He's becoming impossible to live with, his resentment is devouring him, and ruining his health to boot. What will happen to him if he isn't cured of this disease?

Ben's boss, meanwhile, isn't losing any sleep. His conscience is clean. He's not even aware there's anything wrong with the way he treats his subordinates. In fact, he's noticed some of the people in his department are very hard to get along with. Especially Ben, who seems to be so negative all the time. He's not sure he'll be able to keep him on staff. . . .

Who is going to suffer more from Ben's resentment – Ben or his boss?

Freeing Yourself of Resentment

The remedy for resentment is as simple as the problem itself: since resentment results from actions which don't correspond to what we expect from some idealized image of a person, all we have to do is change the action – or change the image. If we look at our example, this leaves Ben with two options.

Ben can set to work trying to change the behaviour of his boss by letting him know there's a problem with the way he treats his employees. If no one has ever mentioned anything before, Ben's boss may very well have been acting with the best intentions in the world, in which case he'll be happy that someone has finally been honest enough to bring the problem to his attention.

Try to think of people you know who attract resentment without being aware of it. Don't you think you'd be doing them a service by letting them know there's something wrong with their behaviour? I've known people like this, who have been able to improve their relations considerably after being told what they were doing to upset people.

I've also known people who have refused to change. They think it's other people's responsibility to adapt to them, not vice-versa. It's a question of point of view, and of power. This is where the second option becomes useful. In Ben's case, it's highly unlikely that he'll be able to change his boss's behaviour. So he has to live with resentment, which is pushing him towards an early and unexpected retirement. Or he can work on accepting his boss the way he is. After all, where did he get the idea that a boss has to be understanding, generous, and equitable? Does anyone's boss really live up to this image completely? Does Ben himself practise the virtues he demands from his boss?

You can see that it wouldn't take much to transform these terrible feelings of resentment into a simple disagreement over the way the department personnel should be handled, which would be a lot easier to live with.

Changing a Long-Term Situation

It's possible to change behaviour which causes resentment as it's happening. For example, my neighbour drives me crazy every Sunday morning, cutting wood for his fireplace with a power saw. I can take the necessary steps to get him to stop, or arrange to be absent from home at that time. But what can I do about an injustice that occurred ten years ago, by someone I haven't seen since, but for whom I still feel such resentment it's as if it happened yesterday? Can I do anything to change the original action? No – the harm is done, and there's no way I can go back and demand an apology or compensation. Can I change my image? No – I could never consider what that person did to me as acceptable behaviour. Then what? Am I condemned to live with this ball of resentment to the end of my days?

Your Training Programme

Fortunately, situations involving verbal ping-pong, and people you find difficult because of resentment are both fertile ground for putting counter measures into practice. The following training programme can help you to alter your interpersonal relations.

Exercise: Working on Resentment

First, take a sheet of paper and make a list of all the people you know or have known against whom you feel even the slightest resentment.

Next, for each person on your list, answer the following questions:

- What is the cause of my resentment towards this person?

- Which of my expectations have not been fulfilled by this person?
- How can I put an end to my resentment (change my image, satisfy my demands, etc.)?

Write down your answers – then *put them into practice!*

Cleaning Up Communication

One way to be sure of getting involved in verbal ping-pong matches is not to take care of your responsibilities, however minor they may appear. By accepting a responsibility you create an expectation, and by not taking care of it you are provoking feelings of frustration. Here are some areas which may be sources of frustration for others, and which you can easily do something about:

- Take care of all outstanding communication (messages you didn't send, letters or thank you notes you 'forgot' to write, visits you promised to make and didn't, etc.).
- Make apologies for all responsibilities or engagements you didn't keep (returning a book, helping with the housework, etc.).
- Clear up any imprecise, vague areas in your communication (you forgot to mention a pay rise, or that you took someone out for dinner, etc.).
- Stop being secretive, telling lies, and pretending about things in areas where you feel confident enough to show your vulnerability.

Preparing for Reconciliation

Here is a way to approach a meeting with someone to reconcile your differences. By writing down the things you want to say, you won't forget anything in the heat of the moment:

- Clearly explain your fear of rejection.
- If the other person refuses to open up to you, explain your feelings in detail.
- Speak using the first person – 'I' – to make it clear you're talking about yourself only.
- Above all, don't try to read the other person's mind; don't put words into their mouth. There's nothing more exasperating than listening to someone say, 'Oh, yes, I know exactly what you're thinking . . .'
- State clearly that the friendship or affection you feel for the other person is not being questioned.
- Finally, recognize your own failings and weaknesses, and show the other person you are vulnerable.

Learning to Forgive

Real forgiveness is a feeling of acceptance. It isn't simply a question of forgetting or negating the sufferings and wrongs of the past: real forgiveness means remembering serenely and harmoniously without experiencing any negative emotion.

Being able to regard past events calmly and serenely requires an inner transformation which is very difficult to realize on your own, without any outside assistance. The process I am suggesting has to be done in a state of deep relaxation, which this book teaches you in Appendix 3.

6

Four Important Stages

We often have to deal with people whose negative personalities cause problems for us: a boss who suddenly blows up about some minor error; a shopkeeper who refuses to help you; a partner who has been suppressing frustration all day and blows off steam at you . . .

Whatever types of difficulties you encounter, you need a strategy to deal with them effectively, and a way to transform difficult situations into occasions for success instead of failure. The following strategy was developed by an American psychologist, and I can vouch for its effectiveness personally. It consists of the following four stages:

1. Evaluate the situation.
2. Stop trying to change other people.
3. Learn to distance yourself.
4. Adopt a strategy and apply it.

A fifth stage in the process might be to anaiyze the results of your behaviour after the programme has been put into practice, which would allow you to modify your strategy depending on how well it succeeded.

Evaluate the Situation

As we've seen, difficult behaviour can be the result of negative circumstances in a person's life at that moment. As we tend to blame other people for their faults very quickly, the first thing you have to do is to make sure you're really confronting a difficult case. If the situation is unclear, you need to ask yourself a few questions. In that way you can avoid blaming yourself later for having made an incorrect assessment. We'll examine the questions one by one.

Is This Typical Behaviour?

One way of finding out is to discover what triggered the conflict; if you're honest with yourself, you won't have any trouble putting your finger on the exact words or gestures that led to the conflict. This will allow you to judge whether the conflict started with you or with the other person. You can also check to see if the same circumstance always triggers off the same effect, and if it occurs frequently. For example:

Jeanette and Charles are biologists who have been chosen to work on a research project together. From the start Jeanette decided her colleague was morose, and didn't have the qualities necessary to work effectively on a demanding project. After two weeks, Jeanette is at the end of her rope. Not only is Charles socially inept, but he also refuses to share scientific data with her. The atmosphere in the small lab where they spend entire days together becomes unbearable. Jeanette finds it harder and harder to sleep, and her work begins to suffer.

Finally, after an out-and-out argument with Charles, Jeanette decides to get to the bottom of things. She discreetly questions other colleagues who know Charles, and tries to find out about his past behaviour. Each time he becomes negative with her, she writes down the circumstances that provoke the conflict. Her efforts are rewarded. In less than a week, Jeanette has managed to create a composite portrait of the way Charles behaves.

Charles had asked for a transfer shortly before being assigned to the project with Jeanette, and his demand was refused. Charles received his degree at a university that was much less prestigious than the one Jeanette went to. When Jeanette joined the company, word soon got around that she came from a top university. This led Jeanette to conclude that Charles was disappointed by his superior's decision to refuse a transfer. On top of that, being forced to work with the 'genius' of the company threatened his self-image, which had already been tarnished by the recent rejection. Having evaluated the situation in this way, Jeanette decides that Charles's behaviour is due to circumstances, and is not a permanent part of his personality, as would be the case with a truly difficult person. This gives her the courage to confront the problem openly. She has a frank talk with him and makes it clear she doesn't intend to allow the situation to continue – she won't be the target of his ill humour, since she is in no way responsible for its cause. In a short time, Charles discovers that Jeanette is the best biologist he's ever met, and their work together proves extremely gratifying.

It is essential to analyze the situation yourself. Do what Jeanette did – write down the events that result in the conflict. You'll soon see a pattern or a series of behind-the-scenes circumstances that will shed light on the difficult situation.

Are You Over-Reacting?

There are some situations that just seem to do it every time – situations that we can't tolerate, that drive us so far up the wall we finally explode in a burst of uncontrolled anger to the astonishment of others. Such excessive reactions produce feelings of immediate dislike for someone, make us get irritated over trifles, or be unnecessarily rude. In *our* mind, it's the other person, or people, who are being difficult. How do we appear to them?

You've probably noticed that when you develop a dislike for someone, their slightest word or gesture becomes irritating. If you have this tendency, then you'd better be honest enough to admit it. Instead of insisting that other people be less difficult with you, try to be a little easier on them! Analysis will help you to evaluate whether you're over-reacting, or whether your reaction is justified. To do this, try the following.

- Look through a journal, or search your memory for relationships of this kind you've experienced. If you fall into this category, you won't have much trouble, since this type of difficult relationship is often profoundly disturbing, and not easily forgotten.
- Make a list of these people. If there's someone in your life at the moment who fits the description, use them as a subject for this exercise.
- Dig deep in yourself and try to find the reason why you find them so hard to take. When did you start to feel disturbed in their presence? What exactly bothers you about them? Their attitude? Lifestyle? Voice? Personality? Way of dressing? Laughing?
- Try to recall your own reactions, and what set them off.

Will a Frank Discussion Clear it Up?

This is the third question Jeanette asked herself once she had discovered the underlying causes behind Charles's negative behaviour, and was able to identify her own role in the situation. If you find yourself facing a person who like Charles has been embittered by personal disappoint-ments, frustrated ambitions, professional conflicts, etc., it's possible to overcome the barrier between you without damaging either the other person or yourself, and at the same time assert yourself. Here's what to do:

- Ask for a meeting. If necessary, set a definite time and place. Try to make sure you won't be interrupted, and show the other person you take the problem seriously.
- Start the discussion by stating you believe the situation between you isn't clear; something's definitely wrong.
- Wait for their reaction.
- Depending on the way they react, determine what type of difficult person you're dealing with. (You may want to read over the first few chapters of this book to refresh your memory.)
- Be diplomatic! For example, Jeanette didn't come right out and say,

'Oh, I know all about what happened with your job transfer, and your insecurity.'
● Above all, don't be condescending or arrogant.
● Finally, something we can't repeat often enough – *don't try to read the other person's mind.*

Here's how Jeanette might have got the conversation going:

'I feel there's some tention between us, and it's beginning to affect our work. I don't have as much as experience as you do, and I was hoping to learn a lot and improve my methods by working with you. But that's not happening. Do you think we're just incompatible? I'd like to know what you think about it.'

Stop Trying to Change Other People

We possess an extraordinary capacity for creating illusions about the people around us, especially about those we love. Although we often love people despite their faults, it's often because we hope someday they'll change and conform more closely to our desired image of them. Finally the day comes when we realize changing another person is beyond our powers – especially if the change we want runs counter to their own will. When that day comes, we either start loving the person for who they are, or we stop loving them altogether – that's where the danger lies.

This is not to deny that we have the capacity to change. Every human being evolves throughout the course of their existence. The environment causes us to change, as does individual will, and this continues to very old age. But it's during the first twelve years of life that we are most malleable – yet even then we have the utmost difficulty getting our children to conform to our wishes. Once we reach adulthood, our evolution is almost completely beyond the conscious control of anyone else.

Wishes are not Reality

Try to remember the last time you had an unpleasant or painful encounter with someone, and said to yourself, 'If only he were less nervous!' or, 'If only he were a little more tolerant . . .', or 'If only my children were less selfish . . .' and so on. Our error consists in believing that others should conform to our desires. And when they don't, we blame them for it. We label them difficult or intolerant, selfish or demanding, and so on.

The important thing is to realize we're dealing with real human beings, and that *every* person has qualities and faults. Other people are not creations of our imagination – we can't eliminate aspects of their personalities that don't live up to our expectations, nor can we give them qualities we think they should possess. That's why I'm so pleased whenever someone tells me I've disappointed them. To me, this means the person hasn't been in touch with who I really am, but with a projection of who they think I am – in other words, with themselves.

You Can Influence People's Attitudes

The intelligent thing to do is to become conscious of the reality of the people around us, both of those who please us, and those who don't. We can also contribute significantly to their happiness and self-fulfilment, if that is what they wish. While you may do your utmost to improve a situation between yourself and a difficult person, you should under no circumstances attempt to modify their personality. You won't succeed, and it won't be of any use. The only thing you can do is to modify their attitude towards you. By bringing the problem or conflict out into the open, you help the other person to see themselves more clearly – just as you're now able to see yourself better.

It's by becoming aware of the forces, desires, and repulsions that make us act in certain ways, that we are better able to take control of our lives, assert ourselves, and attain fulfilment.

Learn to Distance Yourself

As we'll see in more detail, it's indispensable to learn how to protect yourself from the damage difficult people and conflict situations can cause. When faced with a difficult relationship, we tend to get deeply involved; we lose all sense of objectivity; our day-to-day lives are soon affected, as we become preoccupied with the problem – we may even become obsessed by the difficult person, and the problems they are causing. This is what happened to Jeanette. Overwhelmed by her problems with Charles, she became unable to sleep and couldn't do her work properly – until she took hold of herself and analyzed the situation objectively.

But keeping your distance from someone who exerts a strong influence is easier said than done. Difficult people seem to know how to trigger negative emotions – just what to say or do to make us upset. That's why we've dedicated an entire chapter to techniques to help protect you, and which will allow you to remain detached.

Adopt a Strategy and Apply It

In your exchanges with difficult people, there are only two types of strategy to choose from: either you get involved in a power struggle with the aim of coming out on top, or you look for a way to achieve satisfying results while taking the other person's needs into account.

As we've seen in previous chapters, there are different types of difficult people, so it follows that our strategy will depend on the type of attack you are subjected to. When we look at the world around us, we see there a struggle for survival, where the big fish swallow up the little fish, and the strong dominate the weak. There's a great temptation to consider our relations with difficult people as a struggle, where the aim is to gain the upper hand. However, you've probably noticed that we have avoided suggesting that this becomes the main objective of your training.

Avoid Win–Lose Situations

Whenever you have a win–lose situation, the loser won't rest until they have found some way of getting revenge. But if you think about it, although the animal kingdom relies on a balance of strong and weak, nowhere do we see a weak animal waiting patiently in order to exact revenge on another animal for a past humiliation. This is a characteristically human trait, which, as we know, results in all kinds of disasters: wars, famine, repression, needless destruction, and so on.

This is why we aim at restoring communication at the point where it breaks down, and defining your position, as well as the other person's, if necessary. Not letting someone walk all over you doesn't necessarily mean dominating them – it means not letting them dominate you, and, based on this affirmation, doing something constructive about the situation.

The Win–Win Attitude

Another way to approach our relationships is to try to produce a situation that satisfies our needs as well as the other person's.

In Chapter 5 we analyzed the process whereby we accumulate negative points each time we come out a loser in a relationship. When we win, we score positive points. There are people for whom we feel no special sympathy who surprise us with the generous things they do for us. Each time we feel like a winner in our relations with them, we are consciously or unconsciously scoring a golden point in their favour. The day may come when they do something that tips the scales, and we experience an immense feeling of gratitude towards them.

Winning by forcing someone else to lose ultimately means setting yourself up to lose out as well. We're all in the same boat, and if I make a hole because I want you to sink, I'm eventually going to sink too. The choice of being a winner by making others losers is not a real choice at all. The real choice is that either we both win together, or we both lose together. That's why we must develop a win–win attitude.

You Have a Choice

You have the choice of either creating a relationship based on force and domination – a relationship bound to fail eventually – or to look for a way to satisfy both parties. When faced with a difficult person, you have to be very clear in your mind as to what strategy you intend to use: are you going to try to crush the other person in order to experience the pleasure of victory or revenge? Or are you going to protect yourself and then look for ways to establish a constructive dialogue? These two options are always available to you. The only variable is your choice of approach.

Becoming Aware of Negative Interaction

The main problem with applying a win–win approach is that the negativity which characterizes the communication can easily engender more negativity in you – the old vicious circle. Sometimes we're so upset and exasperated that any possibility of improving the situation, or bringing it to a positive conclusion, seems very remote. When you're the target of anger, slander or injustice, it can feel all but impossible to control yourself and not react in kind. However, if you wish to assert yourself, improve the situation, and help the other person all at the same time, then you have no choice. You must learn to control the way you react in order to break the vicious circle and set up a cycle of positive interaction.

In order to defuse conflict situations and start communicating with difficult people you must respond to anger with patience, to disdain with respect, and to harmful intentions with benevolence. If you think that this is a superhuman task, the simple fact that you've read this far is sufficient proof that developing such reflexes will not present much of a problem for you. All you have to do is practise the exercises suggested later on.

Strive for Positive Interaction

Here's some good news: in the same way that negative attracts negative, positive attracts positive – the hard thing to do is to reverse the current. We've analyzed how difficult people seem to have the capacity for bringing out the worst in us, so we find ourselves doing the very same thing we've been criticizing them for doing. However, as difficult as a person may be, they still are capable of responding positively to the right kind of stimulus; everyone (almost) possesses the necessary resources for becoming an open, positive, and communicative person.

Conditions for Success

To start the process, you must categorically refuse to participate in any destructive games. Then, when attempts to involve you in such games cease, you can start being the engine that pulls the relationship in a positive direction.

For example, say you're ready to play win–win with your steamroller boss, your incisive colleague, your whining spouse, and your neighbour the clam. Whatever they say or do, you won't let it get to you. You're in the perfect frame of mind; be firm and you'll succeed. But please, don't make your task more difficult than it already is by choosing the wrong moment: make sure your subject isn't under any excess pressure or specially vulnerable at the moment because of undue stress caused by overwork, illness, serious personal problems, and the like. If you don't, you risk upsetting the delicate balance the person is trying to maintain in order to get through a difficult time. You'll meet with much more resistance than at other moments, and your attempt will probably fail. However, after the crisis has passed, the same people may show themselves ready to change.

There are two lessons to be learned from this: first, you can't force things; next, don't get discouraged because you don't succeed on your first attempt. It may just be an indication that the time isn't right.

Of course, you shouldn't be under any excess pressure either. In order to bring your operation to a successful conclusion, you will have to draw on all your resources of patience, understanding, and adaptation. To do this, you too must be in top shape. This may seem obvious, but you'd be surprised how frequently we show signs of being under excessive pressure without even knowing it. Make sure you analyze your own situation first. If you've undergone a serious crisis in the last few months, wait until you've regained your sense of equilibrium. If you don't, you won't have the energy to deal with the situation properly. Take care of yourself, then deal with others . . .

Another good precaution to take before confronting a difficult person is to think about what you will do if your efforts fail. Ask yourself what the worst possible consequences would be if you didn't try to rectify the situation. Write this down in your notebook to refer to later when you evaluate the effectiveness of your actions. Now ask yourself what other solutions might work in case your first attempt doesn't.

There's nothing worse than feeling caught in a trap, especially since the trap is not a real one. We're never condemned to live with somone whom we find impossible, or to work for or with some who makes our life a living hell. There's always at least one, and usually a number of, alternatives open to us. If you don't think you have any alternatives, you'll always find yourself with your back to the wall. The very fact that you're so anxious to get results will seriously reduce your chances for success. On the other hand, if you have other options, you will be more objective in the face of an initial failure, and much more effective.

You may ultimately decide that leaving things as they are is preferable to making another attempt at reconciliation. You have every right to withdraw, and leave the difficult person to their own devices. The pro's and con's must be evaluated carefully before taking any action. You should be aware of the risks you're taking, the dangers involved, and the possible consequences. Once you've done this, forget about your doubts, and concentrate all your efforts on the positive effects you wish to produce. The difference between winners and losers is that losers think about what they're afraid will happen, while winners think about what they *want* to happen.

7

The Positive Power
of Words

Words are weapons. They can cut as deeply as a knife. The scars they leave are less visible, but they are just as painful. But words are also instruments of healing and pleasure. They can be used to calm someone, to carry on a dialogue, and to negotiate. In previous chapters we've been looking at ways to defend yourself against attacks while remaining calm and in control. Now let's round off some of the techniques you've been exposed to, in order to help you avoid abusing words, and to pave the way for fruitful negotiations.

Three Commandments of Defence

Using words to defend yourself requires an understanding and mastery of three basic principles:

- Recognizing an attack.
- Adapting your defence.
- Carrying your defence to the end.

Recognizing an Attack

Some attacks are obvious. When an angry driver jumps out of his car with his fist raised and rushes towards you screaming abuse, you can be pretty sure you're dealing with a verbal attack that could turn into a physical one. Under other circumstances we may think we're being attacked when we aren't. Some people are short-tempered and easily offended, even though they have the best intentions in the world. If you're one of these people, take care not to see harm where in fact there is none. Finally, some attacks are so well disguised they don't appear to be attacks at all. This may seem unimportant if we consider that an attack only becomes troublesome when it affects us, and that if we don't notice it, it can't be affecting us! However, there's a useful Chinese proverb which says, 'Water droplets can do more harm than a violent storm, because they will eventually split the hardest rock, while the storm leaves it intact.'

Verbal attacks may not be recognized, either because they're well disguised and subtle, or because they come from people with whom we think we have a positive relationship, for example:

Mary has a nineteen-year-old daughter, Louise, who is a pleasant, good-natured adolescent, with a kind heart and winning smile. On a few occasions Mary has noticed that Louise has come home in a bad mood. She seems troubled, and on the point of breaking into tears at the slightest provocation. After further observation, Mary is able to relate Louise's mood shifts to when she goes out with her best friend, Carol. But when questioned, Louise insists she and Carol are still best of friends.

Mary is determined to get to the bottom of things. She observes Carol whenever she comes over to the house to visit Louise, and soon realizes that her daughter is being victimized by Carol, without being aware of it. During their conversations, which appear outwardly friendly, Carol constantly pricks at Louise with sharp little verbal attacks, so subtle as to be almost imperceptible. Louise, however, has no idea she is the target of a constant flow of verbal abuse.

For example, Louise is a little self-conscious about being thin, but it didn't bother her until Carol calmly announced, 'I bought my dress for the party. It's really low-cut. Of course, not everyone can wear that kind of dress.' In this way Louise is being gradually poisoned by her relationship with Carol, without knowing it, which is what lay behind her apparently inexplicable mood changes.

This type of attack falls into the cutting remark category. While it is more subtle, and therefore harder to detect, than some other types, it's just as harmful. The lesson here is that you must at all costs protect yourself against toxic people, and refuse to make them a part of your circle of friends and acquaintances. Either let them know they will have to change their behaviour, or distance yourself from them right away.

Adapting Your Defence

You have to learn to adapt your defence to the type of attack being levelled at you – not only in terms of quality, but also intensity. It would be useless to expend a lot of energy reducing an unskilled adversary to tears. In the first place it would be cowardly, and in the second place, your aim is not to destroy someone but to respond in a way that will be helpful.

We are all capable of affirming ourselves without crushing other people. Unfortunately, many refuse to understand this simple principle. For example, 'If you really loved me, you wouldn't be such a spendthrift', a husband tells his wife. The woman, using one of the techniques you read about earlier, could say something like, 'Isn't it interesting that so many men are under the impression that their wives don't love them. . . ?' The confrontation could, and should, end there. The husband will no doubt be surprised by his wife's objective reaction, and probably change the subject as soon as possible.

On the other hand, the wife could have responded quite differently: 'It's really interesting that a lot of men, once they've reached your age, start thinking their wives don't love them any more.' With that little dig, she gets her revenge. If you give in to this type of temptation, you can expect the argument to continue, and you should make sure you are sufficiently 'armed' to counter any subsequent attacks. If you're dealing with someone close to you, this type of counter-attack will probably lead to a session of verbal ping-pong. It's much better to avoid this, because sooner or later you'll pay the price.

Carrying Your Defence to the End

Defending yourself against a difficult person may require being hard and incisive. If you're not used to acting this way, you may start feeling guilty, become indecisive, and cut your efforts short half way through. Verbal self-defence isn't an incitement to violence. On the contrary, its aim is to put an end to the violence being perpetrated against you. It allows you to affirm yourself and get what you want without having to resort to force. So don't stop half-way through, and don't allow your surprise to paralyze you. Be firm and energetic!

The Most Frequent Types of Attack

We've already seen a few examples of the different kinds of attacks launched by difficult people. In this chapter we offer more examples, classified according to the precise type of attack they represent. You can use them to plan and prepare your counter-measures. First, let's look at the two main types of subtle attack.

Disguised Accusations

Disguised accusations are the easiest kind of verbal attack to disarm, as long as you're able to stay cool. Here are the most common types. With a little practice you'll be able to recognize them immediately.

Type A: 'If you really . . .'

- *Adolescent to parents:* 'If you really wanted me to do well in school, you'd buy me a computer . . .'
- *Spouse to partner:* 'If you really loved me, you wouldn't talk to me like that . . .'
- *Teacher to student:* 'If you really wanted to pass your exam, you wouldn't skip every second class . . .'
- *Doctor to patient:* 'If you really wanted to lose weight, you wouldn't eat so many sweets . . .'

Each of these disguised accusations implies something:

- 'You don't care whether I do well in school or not . . . therefore you are bad parents.'
- 'You don't love me because you don't show any consideration for me.'
- 'You don't want to graduate.'
- 'Either you don't care about your weight, or you haven't got enough willpower.'

A variation of this type of disguised aggression, which uses an impersonal accusation, is slightly more subtle, but its effect is the same:

- 'Parents who care about their children wouldn't think twice about buying a computer . . .'
- 'When you love someone, you don't use that tone of voice . . .'
- 'A student who wants to graduate doesn't skip every second class . . .'
- 'A person who really wants to lose weight doesn't fill themselves with sweets . . .'

Type B: 'Even . . . should . . .'

- *Good skier to beginner:* 'Even a beginner should be able to take this hill . . .'
- *Patient to nurse:* 'Even a nurse should realize when someone is suffering . . .'

Finally, two remarks that really hit below the belt, but which, unfortunately, husbands and children are expert at using:

- *Child to mother:* 'Mother, even *you* should be able to understand that I need some new summer clothes . . .'
- *Husband to wife:* 'Even *you* should be able to learn how to drive a car properly . . .'

This type of disguised accusation is more lethal than the first. It implies much more than it seems to, and in fact represents a series of attacks, one on top of another. So we decode the messages we find:

- 'Beginner skiers aren't very smart. If you can't go down this hill, it's because you're totally inept.'
- 'You don't have to be smart to be a nurse, but you're even less intelligent than other nurses.'

The attacker is perfectly aware of what they're doing. The intention is to cause harm, to make the person react in a negative way, to show their own superiority, and to place the other in a no-win situation. This is the moment to remember the three golden roles of defending yourself against attack:

- Don't respond to aggressiveness with aggression.
- Think and breathe deeply.
- Throw the aggressor off guard by not getting upset.

The only way to master the weapon of words is to practise defending yourself in win–lose types of games. (See Appendix 4 for suggested responses.)

Example of Type A Response: 'If you really . . .'

Child to parents: 'If you really wanted me to do well in school . . .'
Parent: 'Now, now. When did you start thinking I didn't want you to do well in school?'
Comment: Note the literal interpretation of the child's statement. The parent expressly ignores the second part.
Child: 'Because you won't buy me a computer! All my friends have one . . .'
Comment: The child is forced to show his/her hand, to admit they want a computer because all the other kids have one.
Parent: 'Can you tell me how a computer is going to help you to do better in school? For example, how are you going to use a computer during your exams?'
Comment: Once again the parent takes what the child says completely seriously, and pressures the child to offer more explanations. The child can no longer complain that the parent doesn't care. In this way, the disguised blackmail has been neutralized.

Exercise: Your Turn

Spouse A to spouse B: 'If you really loved me, you wouldn't talk to me like that . . .'
Response by spouse B:

Spouse A:

Spouse B:

Professor to student: 'If you really wanted to graduate, you wouldn't . . .'
Student:

Professor:

Student:

Doctor to patient: 'If you really wanted to lose weight . . .'
Patient:

Doctor:

Patient:

Example of Type B Response: 'Even . . . should . . .'

Expert skier to beginner: 'Even you should be able to . . .'
Beginner: 'Oh, that makes me feel better! You mean even someone as inept as me is capable of getting down here?'
Comment: The beginner at first seems to be calmly repeating what the expert said. They then show they are fully aware of the expert's condescending tone.
Expert: 'No, no. That's not what I meant . . .'
Comment: The expert could have tried to get out of it by saying something like, 'No, you misunderstood me. All I was trying to say is that this is a very easy hill.' But the surprise effect worked, and they are at a momentary loss for words.

Or:

Beginner: 'It's okay, a lot of people are like that. Once they get good at something, they think anyone who can't do it is just stupid. But I didn't expect that kind of thing from you.'
Comment: One of the best ways to respond to this type of accusation is to shift the issue to an impersonal level.

Exercise: Your Turn

Patient to nurse: 'Even a nurse should understand when someone is suffering . . .'
Nurse:

Patient:

Nurse:

Child to mother: 'Mother, even you should realize I need some new summer clothes . . .'
Mother:

Child:

Mother:

Husband to wife: 'Even you, my dear, should be able to learn how to drive a car properly . . .'
Wife:

Husband:

Wife:

Appealing to Emotions

At first glance, this type of verbal attack is not as harmful as disguised accusations. Nevertheless, it's embarrassing and often exasperating, and sometimes enough to make you respond with aggression. In general, emotional attacks come from those who are close to you, and who know your weak points. If you want to maintain the relationship, don't counter-attack! Simply defend yourself. Once again, the same rules apply:

- Don't respond to aggressiveness with aggression.
- Take time to think and breathe deeply.
- Throw the aggressor off guard by not getting upset.

You can easily learn to recognize an appeal to emotion because this type of attack always starts in the same way. Here are a few illustrations:

- Adolescent to mother: 'Why don't you ever try to be nice to me?'
- Husband to wife: 'Why do you always try to make me look like an idiot?'
- Parent to child: 'Can't you ever try to please me?'

The phrases 'Why . . . never' and 'Can't you . . . ever' simply mean 'You never . . .' and constitute an admonishment, an accusation, and an appeal for pity. Since this type of attack is common in close relationships, it can quickly develop into verbal ping-pong.

Here are illustrations of correct responses to these three examples:

Adolescent to mother: 'Why don't you ever try to be nice to me?'
Mother's response: 'Well, now, what could I do that you think would be nice? Let's sit down and I'll make you a nice cup of cocoa. We could have a real talk. Would you like that?'
Comment: The mother neutralizes the situation in two ways: first, by doing exactly what the child wants her to do (be nice), she gives him/her the attention they are demanding. Second, what the mother suggests (cocoa and a chat) isn't likely to excite the child a whole lot.

Child: 'What do you mean! That's a stupid idea . . .'
Mother: 'Oh, well, let's not talk any more about it then. It was just an idea. If you don't like it, we'll find something else to do . . .'
Comment: Mother comes out with flying colours: she makes no blunders, and meets with no resistance. She demonstrates her good intentions, and at the same time achieves her goals. No one gets hurt, and the problem is resolved peacefully.

Exercise: Your Turn

Husband to wife: 'Why do you always try to make me look like an idiot?'
Wife:

Husband:

Wife:

Parent to Child: 'Can't you ever try to please me?'
Child:

Parent:

Child:

Conclusions

As you've seen, most verbal attacks are provocations, which also contain negative implications. Consciously or not, the attacker expects you to react in a certain way. What saves the situation is the element of surprise. You can create a win–win situation if you can react in a way that doesn't fit the pattern, and for which the attacker has had no time to elaborate a response.

It's impossible to predict all the situations in which you may become the object of disguised verbal attacks – the examples in this chapter represent the most common variations. (Appendix 4 at the end of the book offers more suggestions on how to respond to the examples given here.) With a little practice, you will be able to recognize disguised attacks as they occur, even if they appear in an unusual form. Whatever form the attack takes, and whatever your response, you can remain in control if you manage to take the aggressor by surprise.

8

Developing Inner Strength

We meet people who are sources of comfort, inspiration, and hope; there are also people who provoke disagreement, anger, and discouragement – the so-called difficult types. Throughout this book, we have suggested ways to help you open a line of communication with these people, reaching behind their shell of silence, or venomous barbs. In order to do this, you need to protect yourself against the wounds that may be inflicted, and to develop your inner strength.

Recognizing Levels of Aggression

When someone uses language against you, which part of you is hurt? Why is it painful when someone opposes you in obstinate silence, or seems to see right through you? When you are insulted, why do you suffer? Answering these questions will enable you to recognize the signs of verbal attack, and to distinguish between the different levels of aggression.

Physical Aggression

On a physical level, there are a number of elements which form parts of our way of communicating. These include images, sounds, and tactile impressions. When we see difficult people in action, we may be impressed by their exaggerated gestures, or intimidated by the volume of their shouting, or even harmed if they attack us physically.

If you're sensitive to sound, a pair of earplugs will allow you to remain comfortable, no matter how loud the disturbances. It is also possible to learn how to remain impassive while someone is standing right in front of you and insulting you. As far as images are concerned, if you're fortunate enough to be shortsighted, remove your glasses! If you have twenty-twenty vision, look at something else – but don't look at the hands, which can be quite frightening. If this doesn't work, you can resort to humour, which we'll be looking at in the last chapter.

Then there is physical aggression proper. Always remember that it takes two to fight; it's very unlikely someone will attack you physically if you do absolutely nothing to provoke it. Simply remaining firm and impassive in the face of aggression will not encourage a person to strike you, unless they are deranged. However, be sure to maintain sufficient physical distance between yourself and the potential aggressor, so as not to be taken by surprise.

All aggression is accompanied by a discharge of negative energy, which you can feel in the pit of your stomach. An offending remark or threat doesn't hurt in your brain, or in your heart – you feel it right in the gut. This may be why we cross our arms when we feel threatened: our arms form a physical barrier between the source of aggression and our centre, which is sensitive to this kind of energy. The same protection is obtained by holding an object in front of your stomach.

Intellectual Aggression

You may become the object of intellectual attacks in your encounters with difficult people. They may ridicule your ideas, or argue with you in a very intelligent way in order to put you at fault, or they may be able to pinpoint the reason or the exception that proves you're wrong; others are expert at bluffing, still others at twisting your words . . .

If you're worried about not measuring up on an intellectual level, then don't get involved in discussions that will leave you vulnerable and exposed to attack. Let the other person demonstrate their erudition, and listen – or at least make a show of listening – attentively to what they say. When they've finished, all you have to say is something like, 'Well, from your point of view, you are certainly correct . . .', implying that you hold a different point of view. Then carry on with whatever you were saying before the attack, as if nothing happened. Or you can say you didn't understand the argument, which places the aggressor in the difficult position of having to explain their point of view all over again – with no guarantee of being understood this time either! – or of just letting it drop. People who practise this type of aggression find it very annoying to have to repeat themselves, because they usually come out looking a lot worse the second time around.

Physical and Mental Aggression

We are most vulnerable on the emotional level; we often feel drained after an encounter with a difficult person. One essential condition for the success of the techniques we've been suggesting is the ability to remain calm during an attack. However, it's very hard to neutralize a negative emotion with another which could act as an antidote. Emotions affect our entire organism, and provoke neurochemical reactions which take time to complete. That's why it's imperative to practise mental exercises and techniques that can help you to control your emotions.

In order to prepare yourself against the potentially devastating effects of emotion, you can resort to 'shields' and to exercises designed to develop your inner strength. We've been protecting ourselves against emotional suffering since childhood. This means that by the time we are adults, many of us have learned completely to suppress our emotional reactions to the point where nothing seems to affect us – we can no longer be hurt emotionally. The problem is that we anaesthetize ourselves against all the positive aspects of human emotion, such as love and affection, as well.

Other people seem momentarily upset when subject to emotional attack but quickly regain their composure. This is the best way to behave when dealing with difficult people: neither too insensitive, nor too vulnerable. The advice in this chapter is meant to reinforce this state.

Some people are extremely sensitive; emotional blows leave scars which take a long time to heal. Even the thought of facing a difficult person makes them anxious, yet somehow they find the courage to do so. This chapter is meant especially for these people.

(The recommendations in this chapter are not meant to help emotionally deprived or damaged people, who should first seek help and try to establish some balance in their emotional lives.)

Why Do We Suffer?

When a sensitive person becomes the object of an emotional attack, what is it that makes them suffer? People suffer because their self-image or self-esteem is threatened.

From childhood we build our personality around a central core, which is the image we have of ourselves. The more solid and positive this image is, the less likely we are to have emotional problems. The more self-esteem we have, the harder it is for us to believe that others do not hold us in high esteem as well, and therefore the harder it is for us to suffer. If our self-image is defective or fragile, we are much more vulnerable to attack.

An in-depth programme for reaffirming your self-image and self-esteem is beyond the scope of this book, which would be difficult to do on your own without personal counselling. However, we can help you to maintain your self-image, and protect it with a series of shields.

You've perhaps been aware that there are certain situations, verbal messages, or even single words that get to you every time, and always in the same way. We've already seen how powerful language can be. We'll now take our analysis a step further to include all kinds of stimuli, including those which are non-verbal and set off an automatic suffering response.

Deadly Gestures and Phrases

Have you ever worked very hard at something, only to feel your efforts were neither understood nor appreciated? Have you ever wanted to show someone something you created only to hold back for fear of being rejected and ridiculed? We've all had feelings, thoughts, and ideas that have been soiled and rejected by other people's comments, gestures, and mocking attitudes. We've all been made to feel stupid, ridiculous or clumsy by our parents, fellow students, superiors, colleagues – and especially by the difficult people we encounter.

What all deadly phrases have in common is that they attack our self-esteem, sometimes seriously. When we expose ourselves by revealing some hidden treasure, we're not always sure of its worth. 'Is the song or poem I wrote any good? Do I dare show it to someone, or should I keep it to myself, in case the person doesn't like it, and says something that makes me feel completely worthless?' Some of the most frequently used deadly phrases are: 'I haven't got time now . . .'; 'That's a stupid idea . . . you know it's impossible!'; and 'Are you serious? You'll never make it! It's already been done. You've got the mind of a child . . .', and so on.

Different people are sensitive to different words and gestures. What may totally demolish your neighbour may leave you cold. What hurts you may hurt only you, and no one else. This is due to the association of words and emotions. Some words immediately provoke a pleasant sensation, others make us feel deeply uncomfortable, without our knowing why.

Think about the insults and other phrases which disturb you the most. They could have something to do with being lazy, miserly, weak, effeminate, past your prime, unreasonable, a failure, and so on. When you discover a word or phrase that hurts you, you will no doubt associate it with a voice, an image, or a feeling which goes back to your past. These words and gestures have been engraved in your file of early negative experiences, and that's why you automatically react to them in such an intense way. For example, say you go purple with rage every time someone suggests you're a failure. The word 'failure' is like the switch on an appliance: someone says it, and you blow your top. What has happened to your free will?

'She slams the door; I get depressed. She says, "Is that it?" and I shrivel up. She says, "You're still tired?" and I get angry . . .'

This person is walking around with a typewriter stuck to his chest – press a certain key and you get the reaction you want, always. Are we all robots or machines, programmed from childhood to react in a specific way? In part, yes. The repetition of certain behaviour engraves positive and negative experiences in our minds, and causes us to react automatically to a given set of circumstances. Some people are so controlled by these habitual reactions that they are like puppets – all you have to do is pull the strings.

Stopping Automatic Reactions

Fortunately, we have the power to change or eliminate our habits. Most people lie somewhere between the puppet and the liberated spirit. We function automatically for part of the time, and gradually gain more control over ourselves as we make progress in our efforts at self-development.

Desensitizing Yourself

The switches that control us do so without our knowing. For example, my wife would slam the door as she left the apartment after a minor dispute. Inevitably I felt like she'd slapped me in the face, and I would dramatize the event to an extreme. I finally realized that this switch was very harmful, since it provoked me into continuing the dispute when what I really wanted was to calm things down. However, despite the fact that I became aware of my automatic reaction, each time my wife slammed the door, I fell into the trap. By the time I realized I'd reacted automatically again, it was too late – the damage was done. This went on until I had the bright idea of asking my wife to repeat the gesture until I was able to neutralize my automatic reaction. After some minutes, I was able to remain totally impassive when she slammed the door shut, and it hasn't bothered me since.

You can apply this technique to deadly phrases, as well. Make a list of all the things you hate to hear. Ask someone in whom you have complete confidence to read them to you. Observe how a word or phrase, once it reaches your brain, sets off a series of involuntary negative emotional reactions in you. Make the person repeat the word or phrase until you're able to hear it calmly, without any negative reaction. When this occurs, you will be free of this particular source of automatic suffering.

Exercise: Re-Programming Yourself

Another way to deal with the problem of negative automatic reaction is to cause the same switch to set off a different, more positive response, in other words, replacing one automatic response with another. Here's how:

- Make a list of situations which you know provoke a negative reaction in you, and which cause you to harm yourself, your environment, and the people around you. Include everything that makes you angry or afraid, or that you want to hide about yourself.
- When the list is finished, study each provocation and ask yourself what disadvantages your reactions have for you. Would it be more

advantageous for you to continue reacting automatically, or to change?

- Now, ask yourself what kind of reaction you'd like to have instead. Write each of these alternatives down.
- Visualize each situation in your mind, and repeat your positive response, using the present tense, as many times as you need in order to make it automatic.

(There is a useful complement to this technique in the section on self-affirmation, a little later on.)

Mental and Emotional Shields

We Become What We Think

Concentrate on pain, and you become that pain. Concentrate on light, and you become luminous. Repeat to yourself, 'This is impossible . . .' and whatever it is will remain impossible; but say to yourself, 'I can do it . . .' and your chances of success will increase a hundred-fold. I can already hear the sceptics, who are thinking, 'Oh, this is just another one of those positive-thinking ideas . . . As if all I have to do to become a millionaire is to think like a millionaire!' If you're one of these people, it's probably because you have a firm belief that 'It won't work . . . it won't work . . .' and so of course it won't.

Psychologists know all about a phenomenon which they describe as the 'cycle of self-reinforcement'. This means that we tend to influence events in a way that's in accordance with our beliefs. For example, take an elderly person who feels they are incapable of using a video cassette-recorder, believing that 'It's too complicated for me . . .' or 'I can't start learning about these things at my age . . .' Say the person gets a video recorder as a gift. You can imagine what happens: despite all the instructions and help offered, and despite a clearly written manual, they can't seem to grasp the principles of how to use it on their own. Finally they say, 'You see, I told you so!'

People have an amazing capacity to fulfil their own prophecies – especially when the prophecies are positive. In such cases, the person's forces are buoyed by hope. There's nothing magic about this. Saying 'I am healthy . . .' isn't enough to cure cancer, but thinking it can help considerably.

We carry around inside us all kinds of affirmations about all kinds of subjects. Some of these can be called beliefs, while others are prejudices or opinions, or judgements. Whatever they are, they were conceived unconsciously. Some of these affirmations have a harmful effect on your capacity to communicate with others and get what you want out of life. Others have a beneficial effect. It is very useful to know that you can create conscious affirmations, which help you to maintain a positive attitude towards the goals and objectives you set for yourself in life. To do this you just have to follow a few rules, which will guarantee their effectiveness, making them powerful and efficient tools.

Creating Effective Affirmations

The rules have been described so many times that we can almost assume most people know them already. Nevertheless, we will repeat them. Let's use the example of an affirmation that is an excellent emotional shield: 'No matter what anyone says or does to me, I am a worthy human being.'

Person. Using 'I' assures that you identify with the affirmation. Saying 'I am a worthy person . . .' establishes this as a true fact for you – which would not be the case if you said something like, 'You have to have courage in order to . . .'

Present tense. Even if the affirmation refers to a future event, it should be formulated in the present tense. For example, if you want to remain calm next time you encounter a difficult person, don't formulate your affirmations as, 'I'll stay calm the next time . . .' because when the situation arises, you'll think, 'Next time, I'll stay calm . . .' (but not *this* time!). Affirmations influence our unconscious, where only the present exists. In order to be effective when and where you need them, they must be conceived and engraved in your mind as if they were valid at the present moment. For example, 'I am calm . . .' or 'I face the situation courageously . . .'

Positive. Another characteristic of your unconscious is that it has trouble differentiating between a thing and the negation of that thing. For example, if I mention the word 'dog' the animal comes immediately to mind. But if I ask you *not* to think about dogs, what's the first thing that comes to mind? A dog! Therefore, if your goal is not to be afraid the next time you encounter an aggressive person, don't formulate your affirmation by saying, 'I'm not afraid . . .' because this instils the idea of fear in your mind. Instead, say something like, 'I'm courageous . . .' *Concentrate on what you want to attain, not on what you wish to avoid.*

Categorical. Your affirmations should leave no room for doubt, so avoid comparative or conditional statements. For example, if you say, 'Whatever happens, I'll be the calmest person around . . .', what happens if someone is calmer than you? Or if you say, 'I am calm if necessary . . .' how can you establish an automatic reaction of staying calm, and a process for evaluating whether staying calm is necessary or not all at the same time? Your unconscious won't be able to handle it. Instead, say something like, 'I remain calm, whatever happens.'

Attainment. Indicate the state you want to attain, not a gradual progression towards that state. If you say, 'I am self-confident . . .' you evoke a feeling you can easily relate to by recalling events in your past where you felt confident. However, if you say, 'Little by little I gain more self-confidence . . .' then your affirmation loses its power because your unconscious cannot measure the qualification 'little by little'. What's more, just because you make progress towards attaining a goal doesn't necessarily mean you will attain that goal. So in reality, you are not offering yourself any real support, but simply a promise of support some time in the future.

Positive emotion. Your affirmation will be stronger if it's charged with positive emotion. Saying, 'I have self-confidence . . .' is fine: it occupies your mind with a positive thought. But saying, 'I am self-confident and I love being with people . . .' is a lot better because it is charged with emotion.

Other recommendations. Affirmations are linked to objectives. For example, say you want to acquire more self-confidence, stay calm in the face of aggression, and preserve your self-esteem despite the attacks you may be subjected to. All these psychological objectives are realistic, and there's nothing that can prevent you from attaining them.

Four Words to Avoid

Be careful not to be too much of a perfectionist when you formulate your objectives. Saying 'I am always calm and benevolent . . .' isn't realistic – you're setting yourself up to not be able to live up to your own expectations, which will only tarnish the credibility of all your affirmations. You have to be realistic, and project a state that can reasonably be attained. Avoid words like 'always', 'never', 'perfectly', 'totally', and so on.

Also be careful to include only yourself in your affirmations. Saying, 'I remain calm and make the other person laugh . . .' will still only affect you, and no one else. Thinking very hard, 'I want him/her to love me . . .' won't make him or her love you! You might even provoke an opposite reaction. This would follow the rule of inverse flow, which states that the more we chase after something, the more it seems to elude us; inversely, as soon as we stop chasing after it, it starts to pursue us!

Putting Your Affirmations to Use

It takes more than just writing an affirmation down to make it work for you. As we know, we are already programmed with all kinds of affirmations that were engraved in our minds a long time ago. To inscribe new, supportive affirmations, we have to repeat them and reinforce many many times. There are a number of techniques for doing this:

- Hang your affirmation somewhere where it is very visible. This way, you'll look at the message and register it often. Don't write more than one message at a time – this will only cancel out any positive effect; work on your objectives one by one. Change the message when you realize you're not paying attention to it anymore.
- Repeat your affirmation in a low voice, over and over again before you fall asleep, and again as soon as you wake up in the morning.
- If you know how to practise visualization, you can use the technique to imagine yourself living out your affirmation. Repeat the visualization as often as possible, until it becomes a familiar part of your thoughts (see Appendices 3 and 5).
- Repeat the affirmation 1,000 times, out loud, without stopping. This has a very strong effect. In addition to engraving the message on your mind, you approach a state of trance, the full effects of which we will discuss a little later on.

Affirmations as Emotional Shields

Affirmations act on their own: once implanted in your unconscious, they automatically produce the desired effect. However, you can also use affirmations whenever you're under intense pressure in a given situation. For example, if you are the object of an especially corrosive type of verbal aggression, you can protect your self-image by repeating the message, 'Whatever anyone says or does to me, I am a worthy human being . . .' This is an emotional shield. You grab on to a positive emotion, which is firmly anchored in your mind, whenever negative emotions (fear, anger, shame, etc.) threaten to take over.

We can't experience two opposing emotions at the same time, nor can we consciously think two thoughts simultaneously. So you can't be happy and afraid at the same time. This phenomenon explains how you can protect yourself against negative emotions during your encounters with difficult people. You can neutralize your negative thoughts or feelings simply by thinking about something else. If you succeed in building a solid defence of positive feelings and thoughts which are able to resist disturbing negative emotions and thoughts, you will become strong and serene, a master of yourself.

The Power of Paradox

You're having problems with your immediate superior. He calls you into his office, and you know that once again you're in for a lecture about all the supposed mistakes you've made, and that you're going to get into an argument trying to defend yourself. In the past, your superior has always been able to throw you off balance until you lost your temper and stormed out in a huff. But this time you've decided you're going to follow the advice offered in this book, and remain impassive, no matter what happens. However, you know that what your superior says is going to hurt you, and you'd love to find a way to avoid being hurt. What can you do?

One possibility is to repeat a sentence like, 'Whatever he says or does to me, I'm still a worthy human being . . .' to yourself before and during the encounter. This is an effective measure, because with this idea ingrained in your mind you can remain neutral in the face of criticism and attack. But this is a purely defensive position, and there may be a more effective way to deal with the situation.

You get to the meeting on time, but your superior makes you wait in the hallway for thirty minutes without giving any reason for the delay. You know he's just trying to exert his authority, and set you up for what's to come. Finally, you're admitted to his office. He's on the phone, and pretends he doesn't see you come in, so you stand there waiting some more. Finally, he tells you to sit down on a low, hard, straightbacked chair, which places you in a distinctly inferior position, compared to his imposing desk and padded armchair. He grills you with an intimidating look, and then begins his attack, assuming you are psychologically vulnerable.

All the manoeuvres described above are aimed at attacking your self-esteem. The person probably sees you as a threat, and needs to reduce you to a state of submission. Showing a lack of respect or getting angry would be a mistake on your part, since this is exactly what the person wants you to do. He knows perfectly well how to exploit your anger in order to destroy you. You find the man mean, petty, and mediocre, yet you've been placed in a position where he has power over you, and over your career. You're fuming at the thought of the trap he's trying to set for you. You're tempted to come down to his level, and respond in kind. But you know this would only make him happy – there's nothing he'd like better than for you to lose control, get angry, and leave the meeting defeated and depressed.

Fortunately, there is an infallible way to respond to this kind of antagonism. Formulate a kind of blessing in your mind, something like, 'May God bless you . . .' It doesn't matter if you have absolutely no belief in God. Neither does it matter that you have no desire to bless the person in question. The thought itself has so much power that it works all on its own. Repeat this sentence in your mind, and at the same time try to evoke hateful thoughts about someone. It's impossible. Remember, you can't think or feel two opposing things at the same time. So you can't bless someone, and hate them simultaneously.

Repeating this, or a similar, formula will change your outlook. You'll cease feeling spiteful or nervous, and although you may be the victim of all kinds of abuse, you'll remain serene and impassive, beyond the reach of petty aggression. And this will serve to upset the other person completely!

The Power of Incantations

You may have seen images on TV of young soldiers throwing themselves fearlessly into the line of enemy fire, chanting the name of God. They seem to be in a trance, and nothing can stop them. The words used in these incantations are often of praise for some divinity, endlessly repeated, to the point where there is no room for doubt, or even for an awareness of one's own identity. This power is not the exclusive property of religion. If you learn to make conscious use of the incantation technique whenever you're faced with verbal or mental aggression, you can protect yourself. The incantation could be an affirmation that you've repeated to yourself a thousand times, and which thus becomes available to you whenever you need it. It could be a series of sounds or syllables, like the mantras taught by spiritual masters.

The Power of Disassociation

Modern psychology has taken over the role of religion in developing techniques to help us increase our inner strength. It proposes that for each difficult situation, either we find ourselves in the situation, and therefore experience the emotions it provokes, associating ourselves with those emotions, or we maintain an attitude of the observer, thereby disassociating ourselves from the experience. The more a person gets involved with an experience, the more they are associated with it, and the stronger the emotions they feel. The problem is precisely that of being too emotionally involved in a situation – too associated – and therefore incapable of taking any positive, meaningful action. The objective is to learn how to keep your distance.

To illustrate the technique, we'll use the example of the nasty boss described earlier. You're sitting in his office, in the chair which symbolizes your inferior position. How can you remain disassociated? The key is your ability to visualize and use your imagination. The most important thing is to be able to play around with your perception of the person facing you. Distance is important – if you're just a couple of feet away, try to move your chair back a little. Now imagine you're looking at the person through the wrong end of a telescope – he looks very small, minuscule in fact, although you're both in the same room.

Problems overwhelm us when we perceive them as being larger than we are. Imagining these problems as smaller than we are simply requires imagining that we are larger than they. If the person you're talking to is your immediate problem, then imagine you're Gulliver, and he is a resident of Lilliput. Your body is immense, his tiny. This simple thought alone will do much to neutralize his power over you.

Another technique is to switch places. Putting yourself in someone else's shoes means understanding what's going on inside their head. It doesn't mean you become the other person, or agree with him. Switching places means temporarily adopting the other person's point of view, and trying to see, hear, and think the way they do. By putting yourself in the other person's shoes, you can discover what it is that really needs to be satisfied in your relations with that person. Other people have the same problems that you do: their intentions may just overshoot their actions. If you make them aware of it, they'll have to say something like, 'I was misunderstood, misinterpreted . . .', or, 'That wasn't my intention, I'm so sorry . . .'

To understand someone, you must know what their intentions are, what value system or criteria form the basis of their behaviour, especially when that behaviour is a problem for you. If you can do this, you're in a position to suggest alternatives which fulfil the person's requirements, and which are also acceptable to you.

But it's hard enough becoming aware of your own intentions. Aren't other people's intentions even harder to determine? No, because it's easier to observe and understand others than it is to observe and understand yourself! We are often blind to certain aspects of our own personality, which are completely obvious to others. Doing this requires an ability to concentrate on someone else and perceive subtle signs, as well as to ask the right kinds of questions at the right time. Mastering these techniques will help a large portion of your communication problems to disappear.

Physical Techniques for Controlling Emotion

Each emotion is characterized by a specific respiratory rhythm. If emotions modify the way you breathe, then if you voluntarily control your breathing you can modify, or control, your emotions. It's long been known that practising deep breathing by filling the stomach and chest cavities has a powerful soothing effect. This kind of breathing is accomplished by relaxing the abdominal muscles and filling first the stomach, then the chest with air, instead of just the chest. This is how we breathe when we're calm or resting – doing it consciously results in our becoming calm and rested. Another way of reducing tension in difficult situations consists in focusing a part of your attention on pleasant physical sensations: being aware of the feel of a chair or table to the touch, feeling the contact of your feet planted firmly on the ground, and so on.

Finally, we know that emotions are linked to hormonal reactions and secretions, which produce all kinds of physical effects – a well-known phenomenon seen in stagefright. An excellent way to control these effects is to practise dynamic relaxation.

Dynamic Relaxation

The principle behind dynamic relaxation is to relax through movement by mobilizing your body to get rid of the excess accumulation of hormones, and especially of adrenalin. You can do this by shaking your head like a dog coming out of water, or by yawning and working your jaw around, or by pacing around until you calm down. You can also do a simple self-massage, which works like this:

> Roll your head around from right to left in a circular movement, stretching your neck. Massage the nape of your neck with your hands. Stretching your neck also stretches your shoulder muscles, and you can massage them too by crossing your hands to the opposite shoulders, and using your thumb and index fingers. These muscles are usually painfully sensitive because of the toxins that accumulate. Knead the muscles on both sides, strongly enough to cause some pain. Then massage with the tips of your fingers. This should make you shiver right down your spine. Lift your shoulders, then relax and let them fall. Breathe in deeply, then breathe out in a long sigh.

Doing these simple exercises before a difficult encounter should relax you sufficiently so you can deal with the situation more effectively, and remain in control of your emotions.

Accessing Your Resources

Each of us possesses the necessary resources to overcome any problem, and take control of our life. We don't need someone to solve our problems for us – we need people who can help us to locate within ourselves the resources necessary to solve the problem at hand. An old Chinese proverb says, 'Give a hungry person a fish, and he'll eat once; teach him how to fish, and he'll eat for the rest of his life.'

Many of our fears and limitations were formed during childhood. For example, you may have been impressed by an authoritarian adult, and felt yourself tiny in comparison. But you continue as an adult to be influenced by authority, as if the part of you that was afraid then is forever linked to the past. To free yourself of this fear, you have to talk to the child you were, the child who is still inside you, telling him or her that you are now a fully grown adult, and she or he no longer need be afraid.

On the other hand, we sometimes exhibit marvellous qualities which seem to be sorely lacking under other circumstances. For example, how is it possible to have the courage to climb a mountain, yet to be unable to sleep because we have to call someone who we know will be argumentative? Where does our courage go in certain difficult situations?

Experiments have shown that only one repetition of an event is necessary for a reaction to become permanent: once you learn to ride a bicycle, you'll always know how to do it, even if you don't touch one for fifty years. In the same way, if you have been a courageous, dynamic, balanced person in just one situation in your life, that's enough for you to continue to retain that quality throughout your life, even if you don't use it again.

The Visualization Exercise 2 in Appendix 5 will help you to call upon your inner resources when you need them.

9

Humour –
The Supreme Weapon

A thief broke into a house and started carting away almost everything he could find. The owner, who was in the street talking to friends, saw the man come and go, loaded with his belongings. He waited a few minutes, then went into his house, covered himself with a blanket, and pretended he was sleeping. 'What are you doing there', asked the thief when he came back for another load. 'Well,' said the man, 'we're moving, aren't we?'

We all know how shared laughter can brighten up the most sombre of days. We've experienced the magic of laughter from childhood on, when our little smiles and acrobatics seemed to cause such joy in those around us. We continued having a lot of fun during adolescence, when almost anything could provoke a round of giggling. We were sometimes accused of being 'childish' by adults who couldn't understand – not to mention those bouts of uncontrolled hilarity that swept us away from time to time, and which no one or anything could stop. However, it wasn't until later in life that we really learned how to make use of humour – to look at situations and events with amused detachment.

The Essence of Humour

Seeing the humour in situations or events helps to take the drama out of situations, and to realize they're only as important as you let them be. Say you lose something valuable. If you consider the loss serious, it becomes a tragedy. If you can laugh about it, it is within your power to see the situation is a comedy. The essence of humour lies in the unreal nature of things. A man goes to open the door of his car. The door handle comes off in his hand. He's so surprised that he remains speechless for a moment. For us, the spectators, his reaction is the funniest thing imaginable, because we know the scene is impossible, that it has been planned. It's funny because someone mistakes an illusion for reality.

Humour vs. Conditioned Ideas

We talk about black humour, but whether black or white, humour always challenges accepted ideas, and plays with the difference or gap between reality and the way it is expressed. Some people totally lack a sense of humour. This can be due to a conscious effort to take everything seriously. You may think that taking things seriously makes you more important, or gives you more credibility. Having a sense of humour means being able to get outside yourself and look at yourself objectively, and therefore not take yourself too seriously – being able to laugh at yourself. This also allows you to deal with serious issues while not identifying yourself with them by maintaining a certain distance or gap, between the issues and yourself. This makes them much easier to deal with, for everyone involved.

Humour usually provokes a smile rather than outright laughter. We rarely experience pure joyous laughter, because laughing is often partly cruel as we are forced to give up some illusion we've been holding on to. However, humour is an immensely liberating force. The moment a painful illusion which has been making us suffer dissolves in a burst of humour, the burden associated with it also disappears.

Using Humour

Your sense of humour is an important resource in your dealings with difficult people. You can use it to take the drama out of situations, and neutralize other people's aggressiveness. Let's look at a few examples of delicate situations where humour can be useful:

- When you want to say no without offending someone.
- If you're obsessed by a problem, and can only think of the usual solution, humour can help you to re-formulate it, and break out of an unproductive cycle of thinking.
- Have you ever noticed how people who spend long hours working against the clock often need to sit around and tell stupid jokes about anything and everything afterwards? This is simply a way of releasing tension – humour acts as a safety valve.
- During a conflict, when negotiations have reached an impasse, humour can clear away obstacles and incite people to move from their entrenched positions. It opens new lines of communication.
- If you want to reach people who have turned a deaf ear, humour can attract attention without hurting anyone.
- If you want to make someone feel comfortable, cordial good humour can overcome barriers of age, education, social standing, diverse interests, and so on.
- If you have to speak in public, humour helps you to relax and to capture people's attention.

We can see from these examples that humour is a precious means of ensuring successful interpersonal relations.

Sharpening Your Sense of Humour

A sense of humour is linked to the ability to play, and is indispensable for any kind of creative thought. To sharpen your sense of humour, you must allow yourself to play. For example, do you consider work to be a punishment, or do you think the ideal kind of work is the kind that's fun to do? Do you think problems exist in order to ruin your existence, or to stimulate your imagination? How much importance do you place on creativity and playing in your life? If you're the type of person who has a hearty laugh at least once a day, then you don't need to read this section. But few people are sufficiently happy or fulfilled, or oblivious enough of their problems, to laugh even as often as once a day. This section is for them.

One thing is certain: humour makes people laugh, or at least smile. You can laugh alone: you've surely found yourself laughing out loud when reading, hearing or seeing something funny. You can make others laugh too, but to amuse others, you first have to amuse yourself. Laughing is contagious, in the same way that boredom or sadness is contagious. It's impossible for you to use your sense of humour if you don't laugh regularly on your own.

Laughing requires the contraction of two main sets of facial muscles: one pulls the corners of the mouth upwards, and the other pulls the lower lip upwards, stretching the mouth. If you rarely laugh, these muscles can atrophy, and you end up with a permanent scowl, even when you laugh. Therefore, you must do some exercises which make use of all your facial muscles. So every morning before you go out, do some facial exercises, using your muscles to make all kinds of grimaces. This will put a smile on your face and help you to stay young. But you can do something even better: go out and take advantage of every occasion you can to laugh.

Avoid Bad News

The world often seems to be on the brink of disaster, and things appear quite desperate. Famine, war, epidemics, assassinations, natural disasters – there's not much to cheer you up! If you want to maintain your capacity to laugh, a wise precaution to take is not to pay too much attention to newspaper articles and television reports about catastrophes, which are exaggerated by journalists to sell their paper. Is it really necessary to allot so much time to news gathering? If you read a newspaper every day, why not start reading it twice, or three times a week instead? You will discover that while being no less informed, the dose of negativity you absorb is greatly diminished.

Laugh Every Day

Finding occasions to laugh or smile when things are crashing down around you is not a sign of cynicism or madness. On the contrary, humour revives the spirit in the shadow of adversity, providing us with a service which is hard to equal.

Distance yourself from morose people, and stay in touch with people who like to laugh, even when problems arise. Go to funny movies. Read funny books, get tapes of comedians, watch your favourite funny programmes on TV. The more you laugh, the easier it gets to laugh! If you concentrate on the funny things in life, what do you think will occupy your mind? Laughter! Forget about doomsdays, and enjoy your life!

Exercise: Cutting Through the Drama

To sharpen your sense of humour, you can apply a few classical methods of creativity in solving your problems.

Start by recalling a difficult situation, either present or past. Describe the situation in writing in a few lines. For example:

'When I returned from overseas after an absence of some years, I started looking for a job. I was called in for a lot of interviews, after which I'd always get a letter saying something like, "We're sorry to inform you that after further consideration you have not been chosen for the position. We will keep your application on file, in case any other positions become available." After a while, I felt like I was walking around with a cross on my shoulders . . .'

Taken at face value, this is a serious, and rather dull, story. How can it be made humorous?

Consider the same problem from various points of view that cut through the drama, that break the problem wide open and allow you to gain some distance. For example, exaggerating. Exaggerate, extend, and dramatize the facts to an extreme. Present them in a disproportionate, monstrous light:

'When I returned from overseas, I found I'd been gone so long, I didn't even know what kind of money was being used.'

Diminish the facts. Miniaturize, reduce, shrink, subtract, and diminish the original facts:

'I started looking for a job, any kind of little job at all. Really, I had no pretensions about finding anything interesting, just some insignificant position that would pay me ten thousand dollars a month, and provide eight weeks paid vacation a year . . .'

Reverse the roles. Imagine that the roles are reversed, that you are the one who is refusing to accept the jobs. You contradict yourself, and oppose everything that seems obvious. In other words, you exaggerate in an inverse sense:

'I was called in by many people who were fascinated with my person. They were insatiably curious, and I tried to satisfy them, at least at first. Soon I started interrogating the interviewers. There was even one who broke down and started crying after two and a half hours, confessing he couldn't stand his job any longer . . .'

Suppress an element of the problem. Place each element of the problem under scrutiny and, ultimately, eliminate it, giving the situation an absurd or burlesque character:

'After a while, I realized I didn't have to work at all, since I was getting along pretty well on the income I received from various sources. But the insane machine was already in motion, and I kept getting calls to appear at job interviews. Even though I had no interest in acquiring the job, I went anyway because I didn't want to be an added source of frustration for the interviewers . . .'

Find unexpected links. We're used to establishing a link between a glass and the act of drinking, for example; or between a door and an entrance to a building. Change these habitual links, and we come up with terms like a musical glass or a door to eternity:

'I would always end up getting a letter which said "You are so skilled that we don't have a job important enough for you." I got so many of these letters that I didn't have to buy any toilet paper for some months . . .'

Now it's your turn . . .

Saying No With Humour

First, humour will help you to gain time. Getting the other person to smile or chuckle gives you time to organize your thoughts and prepare your arguments. It helps neutralize tension and anxiety, both your own and the other person's.

Second, humour prevents a loss of face:

Your superior asks you to stay and work late. You'd prefer to refuse, but you don't want to antagonize him, especially since there are a number of people present. You know he is very quick to lose his temper. So your refusal has to be very diplomatic.

How can you respond?

'I'd really like to stay late, sir, but after seven o'clock I have a tendency to start adding noughts to numbers! If we want to safeguard the interests of the company, it might be better if I waited until Saturday morning to finish the job. What do you think?'

No one has lost face. Everyone in the office has a good laugh, and your superior gets the message, without having any reason to get upset.

Third, humour eases tension. Someone wants something from you which you're not willing to give – it could be your time or participation. You can use humour to ease the tension, and at the same time make the other person understand that your refusal is not a question of bad intentions. This is especially important if you had to refuse the same person before, under similar circumstances. For example:

You're expecting ten people for dinner, and you've set aside the entire day for getting things ready. Someone calls in the morning and asks for a few hours of your time.

Whatever your relationship with the person, you can use a variation of the following technique: 'I know you need me today,' you say calmly, 'and if you can call a caterer and order me dinner for ten, and have it sent over here by seven o'clock, I'd be happy to help you out.'

What you're doing is simply answering a request with another highly unlikely request, which you make a condition for accepting. You have eased the tension that an outright refusal would have created, and you avoid causing the other person to lose face.

Fourth, humour neutralizes aggressiveness. This is perhaps the most important effect of humour. You know how dangerous uncontrolled aggressiveness can be; it can quickly escalate into verbal violence, prevent you from attaining your objectives, and sometimes lead to the loss of friendship, affection and respect of another person. Humour can help you to avoid all that. As soon as you try to be funny, your body relaxes, your expression softens, your face lights up with the flicker of a smile, all of which makes it very difficult for the other person to maintain a hostile attitude. Let's look at an example:

You're in a check-out queue at the supermarket, waiting to pay for your week's groceries. The express till is closed, so you're nice enough to let two people in ahead of you, since they only have one item each. As you're placing your groceries on the counter, a third person comes up and says: 'Would you mind letting me in front? I only have a few things . . .' Your first reaction is aggressive. You'd like to say something like: 'Yes, I would mind! Get in line like everybody else! I've let enough people in already!' Fortunately, you call on your sense of humour for help. You keep placing your groceries on the counter and reply, smiling: 'I was helping a woman deliver quintuplets this afternoon, when I realized I hadn't anything for dinner tonight. I'd really like to let you in ahead of me, but the fifth baby could pop out at any moment, and I really should get back!'

The other person will probably start laughing, despite the fact that you're refusing the request – and the problem is solved without any need for hostility.

Resist Sarcasm

Be attentive to your tone of voice. The same joke can be interpreted as a pleasant attempt at humour, or as derision and mockery, depending on the way it is delivered. Also, never make fun of people. Irony and sarcasm are double-edged swords because they involve you in a win–lose situation, the dangers of which we've already discussed. You risk setting off an escalation of verbal violence, as the other person understands what you're doing and responds in kind.

In the Lion's Den

Even the most charismatic people sometimes have to face a hostile and derisive audience. Say you have some bad news to announce – humour is the only way to get the message across, while keeping your listeners attentive and on your side. Say a speaker is facing an audience which doesn't seem to be particularly receptive. He already knows that the information he's supposed to deliver is not good news. He clears his throat, and begins: 'When I found out I'd be speaking to you here this afternoon, I thought that if I had the wisdom of Solomon, and the patience of Job, I could maybe avoid the fate of Jonah!' By making the audience laugh, he has already won half the battle.

To conclude this chapter, here's a little story that shows how humour can be used as a way to instruct others about more serious matters. One day, a young student asked a teacher, 'Who did best: the man who conquered an empire, the man who could have conquered an empire but didn't, or the man who prevented someone from conquering an empire?' 'I don't know,' the teacher replied, 'but what I do know is that there's something more difficult than any of those.' 'What?' said the student. 'Trying to learn how to see things as they really are', replied the teacher.

Conclusion

Here we are, at the end of the book. Perhaps you read it right through, from beginning to end. If so, I suggest you go back and read it again, section by section. You'll notice a few things you may have overlooked, things you skipped over, without really registering them consciously.

By following the advice offered here, you will experience a gradual lightening and easing of your day-to-day tensions. This is a practical book, which can help you in unexpected ways: you'll gain more self-confidence, other people will understand you better, they'll want to help you instead of hinder you, you'll make more friends, and so on. Dealing with difficult people also means dealing with your own fears – dispelling those old demons, and making your life a harmonious experience that others can share in and admire.

I can only hope that my work will serve to change your life in some positive way – just like mine was – as you apply the techniques for dealing quietly and effectively with difficult people. Now it's up to you. Only you can transform these words into action. Good luck!

Appendices

Appendix 1: Passive Aggression

There's a special kind of aggressive person who you may have encountered before. These people appear to be generous because they don't know how to say no. But because it's frustrating to always say yes when you'd really rather say no, they build up a lot of resentment against people who ask them for anything. This kind of aggression, which is often unconscious, is masked by an edict that goes back to childhood, which says, 'Be polite!' It manifests itself in subtle ways: forgotten appointments, work that is overlooked, lateness, unkept promises, and so on. We call this type passive-aggressive.

When dealing with a passive-aggressive person, you can't just ask for something and take yes as an answer. You have to go further than that:

- Tell the person why what you're asking is important to you.
- Clarify your request by saying, 'Do I have your absolute word that you'll do this?'
- Make the person understand what will happen if they don't keep their word.
- Continue the discussion after an agreement has been reached, and ask the person to repeat what they have to do. Get it down in writing – just a simple three lines is sufficient.
- Don't wait for the deadline to pass. Make sure the person is taking the necessary intermediary steps to fulfil their obligation – 'How's it going? What have you accomplished so far?' Consider these as reminders that the passive-aggressive person needs.

If the person persists in not keeping their word, try behaving in the same way – give the person a dose of their own medicine. For example: get to a meeting forty-five minutes late; pay the person a month late; make a promise, and don't keep it. Then take time to explain why you did what you did. Ask how they felt when you didn't keep your word. Was it pleasant? Well, that's exactly how you feel . . . Then come to a limited and progressive agreement with the person, something along these lines:

- If the person has the least inclination to say no, get them to say it immediately.

- Talk things over at least once a month, or once a week. If there is any delay, you should be informed immediately.

As with many difficult types, the important thing is to express very clearly how you are affected when the person doesn't keep their word, and to reach an agreement together on how to remedy the situation.

Appendix 2: VAS Test

For each of the following twelve situations, circle the one option which you prefer.

1. You have to spend six weeks locked up in an underground bomb shelter. You'll have everything necessary for your survival. You can only bring one additional item from the following list with you. Which do you choose?
A1 A slide projector and a collection of photographs of people, landscapes, works of art, and so on.
B1 A more comfortable bed than the one in the shelter, and a supplementary heater to provide a constant and comfortable temperature.
C1 A compact disc player and a collection of your favourite music.

2. The thing you like best about a fire is:
A2 Looking at the flames.
B2 Feeling the heat.
C2 Hearing the crackling of the wood as it burns.

3. You have attended a fashionable reception. What you liked most about it was:
A3 A piece of your favourite music, played by a virtuoso at the end of the evening.
B3 The extremely comfortable surroundings – soft carpets, sofas, warm lights, etc.
C3 The beauty of the architecture, and the collection of paintings.

4. You're going out for the first time with someone you find very attractive. What you like most about the person is:
A4 Their charming voice.
B4 The electricity when you touch.
C4 Their elegance or physical beauty.

5. What you dislike most in a bed is:
A5 The way it creaks every time you move.

B5 The feeling of crumbs between the sheets.

C5 That the sheets, although freshly washed, are stained.

6. When giving directions to someone you tend to:

A6 Provide detailed verbal descriptions.

B6 Make a sketch.

C6 Accompany the person, or use gestures to point the right way.

7. What would make your work place most pleasant:

A7 Tasteful décor, with lots of plants and colourful prints on the walls.

B7 Background music of your choice, when you want it.

C7 A work table made of some luxurious material that you enjoy touching.

8. Aside from monetary or sentimental value, the gift you'd most prefer receiving would be:

A8 An article of clothing, in cashmere, fur, or silk.

B8 A collection of your favourite music.

C8 A beautiful painting or print.

9. If you wanted to relax, you'd choose:

A9 A whirlpool, a massage, or a sauna.

B9 Listening to a tape of relaxing music or words, in a quiet room.

C9 Contemplating a magnificent landscape.

10. What you find most intolerable about large, over-populated cities is:

A10 The crowds of people on the streets and buses.

B10 The ugliness of the environment: grimy buildings, dirty pavements, etc.

C10 The incessant noise.

11 The thing you find most attractive about a river is:

A11 Refreshing yourself in its cool water.

B11 Closing your eyes and listening to the soothing sound of the water as it rushes by.

C11 Marvelling at the light on its surface, or the water cascading over rocks.

12. When you think about something pleasant:

A12 You see precise images, alive and in full colour, flowing through your mind.

B12 You talk to yourself about whatever it is, as if you were carrying on a conversation inside your head.

C12 You recall or anticipate the sensations of pleasure you experienced at that time.

To find out whether you are a visual, auditory, or sensual type, add up the number of As, Bs, and Cs you circled:

Visual (As):

Auditory (Bs):

Sensual (Cs):

The sense with the most points is probably the one that dominates your perceptions. To be absolutely certain, you'd need to do a more detailed analysis – this test is designed to make you more aware of the differences between visual, auditory and sensual perceptions in people, not to measure those differences accurately.

Visual Types

Visual people select images from their past, which they then use to interpret what is happening in the present. They don't like staring people in the eyes – they prefer looking around freely, or looking inside their minds, or just staring into space. They place more emphasis on colours and forms when describing things than do auditory or tactile people, and are usually very sensitive to the colours in their environment, to neatness around them, and to the beauty of landscapes. Visual people rarely get lost. They retain a mass of interior images, and know how to access these quickly when the need arises.

Auditory Types

Auditory people often carry on an inner dialogue with themselves. They sometimes have trouble making decisions, because these inner voices tend to discuss issues endlessly, without coming to any clearcut conclusions. Auditory people often have pleasant voices, and would choose to go to a concert or listen to some good music when they need to relax.

Tactile Types

Tactile people 'feel' things. They know how to overcome obstacles and resolve conflicts. They often demonstrate conflicting emotions in their own lives: if they don't love a person, they hate them. They insert a lot of pauses when speaking, which gives them time to tune in to their feelings, and establish tactile contact with their surroundings, and with their inner selves.

Appendix 2: Criteria Test

Circle two choices for each of the eight following situations.

1. Which of the following events would you find most painful?
A1 Breaking an object which you value greatly.
B1 Losing important files, which contain important information on a subject that concerns you.
C1 Watching a place you like get destroyed.
D1 Being prevented from doing something you like to do.
E1 Missing an important family or social get-together.
F1 Suddenly losing the friendship of a person you like, for no apparent reason.

2. What is it about past vacations that has made the deepest impression?
A2 The people you were with, or who you met.
B2 The places you discovered, or went back to.
C2 All the enjoyable things you did.
D2 The fact that the vacation date coincides with an important event in your life.
E2 All the interesting things you learned.
F2 The beautiful or valuable souvenirs you brought back with you.

3. You have a choice between six jobs. They all offer the same salaries, vacations, pensions, and social programmes, and are situated at equal distances from your home. However, each has a particular advantage. Which would you choose?
A3 This is the first time in the history of the profession that someone with your background and training has been named for the position. The news causes headlines.
B3 Your office is in an especially prestigious building.
C3 You will be in charge of one, or a number of activities which you enjoy doing, or which interest you for personal reasons.
D3 You'll be working closely with an old friend whom you like a lot.
E3 You'll be provided with very complete information and data, and the latest research techniques.
F3 You'll be provided with highly sophisticated materials and equipment – the best in your field.

4. For professional reasons, you have to leave home to spend a year in an underdeveloped, tropical country. What worries you the most is:

A4 You'll be far from friends and family.

B4 It offers very few of the comforts you're used to.

C4 Nothing important ever happens, and you'll be totally isolated from any great world events that might take place during your absence.

D4 It is so isolated; you won't have anything to do outside of working hours, and will become extremely bored.

E4 You know nothing about the place, and you're afraid there will be a serious lack of information of all kinds.

F4 If you bring your furnishings with you, the bugs will probably eat your carpets, tables and chairs, and the humidity will destroy your paintings and prints.

5. When you think about your childhood, what kinds of memories come most easily to mind?

A5 The exact names of school friends, other precise information about this period in your life.

B5 People who played an important role in your childhood. Aside from your parents, include friends, neighbours, extended family, teachers . . .

C5 Your favourite games, or things you liked to do as a child.

D5 The toys or other objects you possessed that gave you a lot of pleasure.

E5 The place, or places where important events in your childhood occurred.

F5 Memorable events you witnessed or took part in.

6. Your dream is to:

A6 Live among warm and communicative people.

B6 Live in a beautiful place.

C6 Accomplish much more than you do now.

D6 Play a central role in an exceptional event.

E6 Buy all the things you want.

F6 Possess great knowledge, and be universally cultured.

7. The year is 1500 BC. You are a counsellor to the pharaoh of Egypt. You are given free choice to pick one item, dedicated to posterity, that will be buried with the pharaoh in his tomb. What would you choose?

A7 A life-like description of the king's parents, children and friends, describing their qualities, and how devoted they were to their ruler.

B7 A beautiful chest made of wood and gold, inset with precious stones, as a testimony to the skill of the artisans in the kingdom.

C7 A cabinet containing all the medicines known at that time.

D7 A commemorative plaque depicting the splendour of the pharaoh's coronation day, and the main events of his reign.

E7 A painted fresco depicting all the pharaoh's glorious achievements.
F7 An empty underground monument, which would serve as a place of meditation for future generations.

8. You learn about the discovery of a tribe of people hitherto unknown in a remote Himalayan valley. The first thing you want to know is:
A8 How many there are, what they call themselves, what language they speak, how large their territory is, and any other precise information you can find.
B8 How this extraordinary discovery took place – on what date, by whom, and under what circumstances.
C8 What did the tribe's artifacts look like? Will they be exhibited at some time in the near future?
D8 How do these people, completely isolated for so long, behave? Are they friendly or hostile? Curious about the outside world, or fearful and suspicious? What are the male-female relations like?
E8 What does their home valley look like? Do they live well? Will it soon be possible to visit them in their natural setting?
F8 What can be done for them? Is there any kind of organization you could join to help them?

Analysis Table

To find your total add up the letters you circled. The two criteria which gain the most points are the ones which are most important to you:

Events:

Places:

Activities:

People:

Information:

Objects:

Events

For you, life is a succession of events. You can easily remember the dates of things that happened to you. You attach great importance to whatever is a first or last occasion. You seem to intensify circumstances, and herein lies the danger: you may become too preoccupied with isolated events, and forget that life goes on.

Places

The world is made up of places which have special significance for you. You need to know where people you meet come from before you can get to know them. Your environment exerts a strong influence on your behaviour and moods. You form very strong sentimental attachments to certain places. You run the risk of forgetting that our real place is the entire world.

Activities

You see the world as a large playing field. To understand someone, you have to know what they do in life. When talking about yourself, you gladly tell people what you do, or what you don't do. You sometimes get the feeling you haven't accomplished anything, even though you've been very active all day long. You like work that requires mobility and movement, and you prefer sports to reading. You risk becoming an activity addict, or a workaholic.

People

What counts most for you in life is people. You like to be in touch with others, and you're preoccupied with your relationships. When you meet people, you have to know what social group they belong to, if you have any common friends, in order to relate to them. When you have to make a choice, the most important thing is to know what other people are concerned. You may be hindered by your tendency to take things too personally.

Information

There's so much to know! You're always looking out for new things to learn in the situations you encounter, and you're very efficient at collecting data. What motivates you the most is your desire to know more, to obtain all kinds of precise information and general data on a host of subjects. The danger for you is that you analyze things too much, instead of living them fully.

Objects

For you, the world is full of things that will never be fully explored, classified, preserved, and admired. You're very skilful at anything that has to do with objects: organizing, classifying, repairing, building, counting, collecting, administrating, conserving, restoring, etc. You'd make a good manager, since you like things to be in order and in good condition. You value the material side of life. You may tend to see living beings a little too much like objects.

Appendix 3: Relaxation and Visualization

To do this exercise you'll need the help of another person – someone who can read the text to you in an appropriate voice and at the right speed. Or you can use a tape recorder and record the text yourself. Get into a comfortable position – avoid crossed arms or legs. Close your eyes and concentrate on your eyelids, and particularly on the muscles around your eyes. Relax them slowly . . . very slowly. Now let this feeling of relaxation spread to your whole body. Breathe in deeply, and while breathing repeat the number seven over and over in your mind, and imagine you're seeing the colour red. Relax your entire body, from head to toe. Re-lax. Let your body relax completely.

Breathe in deeply again, this time repeating the number six, and visualize the colour orange . . . You only want to do what is good for you . . . Breathe in deeply. Then as you breathe out, repeat the number five in your mind, and visualize the colour yellow . . . Your mind is calm and tranquil . . . Your mind is at rest.

Breathe in deeply again, and as you breathe out repeat the number four in your mind, and visualize the colour green. You are overcome by a feeling of peace. Think of the word 'se-re-ni-ty'.

Breathe in deeply, and as you breathe out repeat the number three to yourself, while imagining the colour blue. A feeling of love grows from deep within you. You feel full of love.

Breathe in deeply, and as you breathe out repeat the number two in your mind, and visualize the colour violet. You are in touch with the real essence of your being . . . You are in harmony with yourself.

Breathe in deeply, and as you breathe out repeat the number one and visualize the colour purple. You are now in touch with the deepest part of your being. Your mind has reached its most profound level. You can use this energy to accomplish whatever you wish, provided that this action is just and something you sincerely desire.

Imagine a large sphere of white light. This sphere is floating above your head, and emits a beautiful golden white light which bathes your entire body. Let the light penetrate and fill you completely. The golden light fills you, and surrounds you and protects you. Only beneficial things can happen to you now. You release all the negativity and resentment, which is being flushed out of your system.

Visualize yourself in a peaceful, natural setting. Experience a feeling of great tranquillity and harmony with your surroundings. What colours do you see? Fill your lungs with sweet smelling, fresh, pure air. Listen to the sounds. Maybe you can feel the heat of the sun on your skin, and the soft earth beneath your feet. You see a path leading away into the distance . . .

Start walking on the path, attentive to everything you perceive:

images, sounds, sensations. The path continues through a forest, and then opens onto a clearing that stretches off across a golden field, as far as the eye can see. In front of you is an area enclosed by a stone wall or wire fence. There is a sign hanging on the fence, with the word 'dump' printed in large letters.

Push open a gate and walk in. You examine a pile of garbage. It looks very old. You bend down and take a closer look, and your eye is caught by a particular piece of metal. Concentrate all your attention on this piece of metal . . . and pick it up. As you hold the piece of metal and weigh it in your hands, think of a time in your past when you stood somebody up – when you said you were going to do something or go somewhere with someone. Do you remember how the person felt when you didn't come through? Do you remember what they said? What did you say or do when you broke the agreement? Now put the piece of metal back where it was and let the memory fade.

Move on to other piles of scrap, looking for other pieces of metal. Pick one up . . . look at it . . . it reminds you of something you did a very long time ago, for which you feel guilty . . . something you knew you shouldn't have done, but which you did anyway . . . Were any other people involved? Did you hurt anybody by your actions? How did you feel? What has happened to your guilt since then? Put the piece of metal back where you found it, and let the memory fade.

Continue walking around the dump. You may be reminded of a time when you were the one who got hurt, when you felt a great deal of resentment towards someone. Maybe you judged or punished someone unfairly, or maybe you were the one judged and punished. You may recall moments of intense hate, anger, sadness, depression. You may think of all the times you were disappointed by others . . . and of all the resentment you feel towards them.

Walking through the dump, you detect a faint but foul odour. You look around, and discover that the smell seems to be coming from a separate part of the dump, enclosed by its own wall. You walk up to the wall, but it's too high for you to see over. You find an old wooden crate, and use it to stand on. What you see on the other side of the wall is a stinking mess of decomposing matter. You realize this smelly heap contains all the things that have been bothering you . . . things you've rejected or hidden . . . your animosity, resentment and hate. You knew these things were there . . . you knew how foul they smelled, and you punished yourself because they were a part of your life. Just be aware of them. The wall hiding this heap of garbage is the same wall you set up between yourself and others . . .

Move off into a part of the dump that's on slightly higher ground. From there you can see beyond its boundaries. You see something in the distance that seems to be shining softly . . . it looks attractive and reassuring. This distant place is surrounded by a halo of blue light, with points of purple and gold. This is where the purest part of your mind resides. But at the moment, there is a pile of garbage between you and this pure place, as well as a wall that bars access to this most profound and positive part of yourself.

Walk away from the inner wall, out through the gate of the dump. You sit down on the ground and look at the dump . . . remembering all the pain, the punishments, the wounds . . . all the judgements you made about others that caused them pain and suffering. It's all there in that dump. Imagine that the dump starts turning slowly at first, then faster and faster, transforming into a huge mass of dark red matter. All your garbage, the fence, the inner wall, the heaps of scrap, blend together into this huge dark red mass . . .

As the dark red mass grows ever more compact, you become aware that it is composed of certain actions you have committed, and of certain things that happened to you . . . but that the mass is not really you. You know there is a much deeper place inside you . . . that place shining softly in the distance – a place of comfort and warmth . . .

From this shining place, a ray of light projects into the sombre mass of your garbage – a ray which stems from your profound desire for reconciliation. The dark red mass grows a little lighter as the ray penetrates. The mass of negative energy becomes orange. As it grows even lighter, you feel that some of the emotions it contains are dissipating, and you feel lighter. The mass of negative energy continues pulsating and getting lighter in hue. Now it turns yellow. You understand that a great number of the negative events you've experienced were steps on your path to understanding – if you hadn't lived them, you wouldn't understand what you do now. They were meant to open your mind, and help you discover yourself . . .

As you think about this, the yellow mass turns pale green. Everything becomes clearer. You understand so much more, and you feel reconciled with yourself. The green colour seems to produce a deep feeling of calm, which pervades your entire body. Reconciliation and forgiveness are easy to achieve. You can now forgive yourself for all the times you judged yourself, and other people, too harshly. And as you experience these feelings of reconciliation and self-forgiveness – as you begin to accept yourself – the mass of negative energy takes on a deep blue colour, warm and welcoming . . . a very beautiful deep blue. Radiating from this blue colour, a great feeling of sensitivity spreads through you . . . and you start to see tinges of purple.

The negativity in the mass before you has almost completely disappeared, and you are getting closer and closer to that inviting place that is your real self . . . the place which has always been there to love you and appreciate you . . . which allowed the dump to exist because it thought you wanted it there. Now that you've made it disappear, your true self embraces you and welcomes you, happy to have you back again . . .

The purple colour turns to gold, with a circle of intensely bright white light, vibrating at its centre. Now the light is distilled even more purely, and becomes invisible. It fills you up . . . your heart fills with pure white and golden hued light. Now send the light to all the parts of your body that need healing . . . to the places where you feel empty, sad, soiled, or hurt. Fill these areas with warm white golden light. Let the light dissolve any remnants of negativity . . . of suffering . . . of need. Let yourself become one with the radiant person you really are . . .

As you let the light fill your body, let it shine all around you as well, radiating from your heart. Let the light of your love spread out around you, outside of you, first touching, then enveloping and protecting everyone you come in contact with. This is how you can spread the grace of reconciliation, in the form of this beautiful light, all around you . . . Now bring your being back to the point where you started out . . . back to the peaceful clearing where you started using your creative imagination and powers of visualization.

I'm soon going to ask you to open your eyes. When you do, you will feel completely awake, and in perfect health. You will feel radiant, and in harmony with life. When you're ready, you can let yourself become more aware of where you are . . . of your presence in this place. Feel the contact of the surface you're lying or sitting on. Wiggle your toes. Tighten and relax the muscles in your legs. Move your mouth. Close your fists slowly. Breathe in deeply. Stretch. Open your eyes when you feel ready. You are fully awake, in perfect health. You feel reborn, you feel charged with renewed energy, and in total harmony with life. . . . Hello!

Appendix 4: Sample Responses

'If you . . . really . . .' (page 76)

One spouse to another: 'If you really loved me, you wouldn't speak to me that way . . .'
Second spouse: 'Do you seriously think I don't love you?'
First spouse: 'It's the way you talk to me that makes me think you don't love me any more.'
Second spouse: 'But what you're saying is very serious. Come and sit down for a moment, and let's talk this over. You have to tell me when you started thinking like this.'
Comment: You'll notice that the second spouse accepts what the first has said at face value, without getting upset or making any protests, which would lead to an unpleasant scene. This way, the bomb is calmly defused.

Teacher to student: 'If you really wanted to graduate, you wouldn't skip every second class . . .'
Student: 'But I can assure you that I really do want to graduate.'
Teacher: 'In that case, why do you skip classes? It's not the best way to do well in school.'

At this point, the teacher is probably getting ready to launch into a sermon, which the student does well to interrupt.

Student: 'I understand what you're saying, and from now on I'll do everything I can to improve my attendance record.'
Comment: Instead of making more or less dishonest excuses, the student only responds to the first part of the teacher's statement, providing a way out of an impending conflict.

Doctor to patient: 'If you really wanted to lose weight, you wouldn't eat so many sweets . . .'
Patient: 'But I really do want to lose weight, doctor, I can assure you.'
Doctor: 'Well, in that case you'll have to pay more attention to your diet.' (The doctor gives a detailed description of an appropriate diet.)
Comment: The patient uses exactly the same manoeuvre as in the previous example. When you feel even slightly in the wrong, as is the case with the student and this patient, this technique is the best way to get yourself out of trouble. You won't have to give any vague, off the cuff explanations, and you assure the other person of your good intentions.

Exercise: 'Even you . . . should . . .' (page 77)

Patient to a nurse: 'Even a simple nurse should be able to realize when someone is suffering . . .'
Nurse: 'You know, what you just said is extremely interesting. Certainly a nurse, with all the training she has, and with all her professional experience, should be able to recognize when a patient is suffering. You're completely right!'
Comment: The nurse took a deep breathe and suppressed her anger. She pretended not to understand that she was being insulted, and totally ignored the sarcasm in the patient's voice. She refused to show she was upset, and created the impression she was really interested.
Patient: 'Oh, well . . . yes, obviously . . .'
Nurse: 'Good. Now how about taking your temperature?'

Child to mother: 'Mother, even you should be able to understand that I need some new summer clothes . . .'
Mother: 'It's quite popular among adolescents to think their parents are

complete idiots. But don't worry about it, you'll get over it in a few years.'

Comment: Once again the intended victim has used the element of surprise to turn things around. The technique consists of shifting the attack to an impersonal level. It usually succeeds in this kind of situation.

Child: 'Mother, you're making fun of me. That's not what I was talking about . . .'

Mother: 'Really? Well what were you talking about. Come and explain to me, so that I can understand.'

Husband to wife: 'Even you should be able to learn how to drive this car properly . . .'

Wife: 'Some men think their wives are idiots, but I'm surprised to see you think that way too.'

Comment: This is still the same technique of depersonalizing the attack. The manoeuvre is non-violent, and ends on a kind of compliment: the husband doesn't belong to the category of crass, unfeeling men who insult their wives in this way. The last part of the sentence implies that the husband may be having a hard time, or that his comment is a simple lapse of character. The wife generously offers him the benefit of the doubt.

If you find it impossible to avoid counter-attacking, for example if the husband becomes excessively abusive and condescending, and the wife wants to put a stop to the insults once and for all, she can always transform her compliment into a cutting remark, as we saw earlier on:

Wife: 'The notion that women are incapable of driving is common to men of a certain age, dear. But don't worry, it's not serious.'

Comment: '. . . of a certain age' is the crucial phrase in the sentence. It could, of course, be replaced by variations such as: '. . . of your generation'; '. . . in your situation'; '. . . of your intelligence', etc.

Exercise: Appealing to Emotions (page 79)

Husband to wife: 'Why do you always try to make me look stupid?'

Wife: 'I have an idea! We'll have a party, invite all our friends. But first you'll make a list of all the things you want me to talk about, and also what you don't want me to mention, so I don't make you feel stupid.'

Comment: The usual technique, in such situations, is to offer a suggestion that will remedy the complaint, but a suggestion you know the other person will refuse. This is exactly what the wife does here. The husband's reaction is predictable.

Husband: 'That's ridiculous. It would be completely bizarre . . .'

Wife: 'All right, let's forget it. It wasn't such a great idea anyway.'

Comment: The subject is closed for the moment. The husband would feel ridiculous insisting in the face of such adamant good will.

Parent to child: 'Can't you ever do anything to please me?'

Child: 'How about trying something? From now on, I'll come and check my homework with you every night. And you can come to all the parent-teacher meetings, so you can get to know my teachers. That way, I'll get good marks, and you can say I did something to please you.'

Comment: Once again, the technique consists of suggesting something that will probably scare the other person off. The child knows his/her parent is already overloaded with things to do, and won't agree to this proposal.

Parent: 'Uh, well, let's talk about it next week, when I have some time . . .'

Appendix 5: Visualization Exercise 1

Here is a visualization exercise to help you put yourself in someone else's shoes. It will also help you to develop your ability to visualize. You will need someone to read it for you in a calm, clear voice, or tape your own voice and then play it back.

Get into a comfortable position – avoid crossed arms or legs. Close your eyes and concentrate on your eyelids, and particularly on the muscles around your eyes. Relax them slowly . . . very slowly. Now let this feeling of relaxation spread to your whole body. Breathe in deeply, and while breathing repeat the number seven over and over in your mind, and imagine you're seeing the colour red. Relax your entire body, from head to toe. Re-lax. Let your body relax completely.

Breathe in deeply again, this time repeating the number six, and visualize the colour orange . . . You only want to do what is good for you . . . Breathe in deeply. Then as you breathe out, repeat the number five in your mind, and visualize the colour yellow . . . Your mind is calm and tranquil . . . Your mind is at rest.

Breathe in deeply again, and as you breathe out repeat the number four in your mind, and visualize the colour green. You are overcome by a feeling of peace. Think of the word 'se-re-ni-ty'.

Breathe in deeply, and as you breathe out repeat the number three to yourself, while imagining the colour blue. A feeling of love grows from deep within you. You feel full of love.

Breathe in deeply, and as you breathe out repeat the number two in your mind, and visualize the colour violet. You are in touch with the real essence of your being . . . You are in harmony with yourself.

Breathe in deeply, and as you breathe out repeat the number one and visualize the colour purple. You are now in touch with the deepest part of your being. Your mind has reached its most-profound level. You can use this energy to accomplish whatever you wish, provided that this action is just and something you sincerely desire.

Imagine a large sphere of white light. This sphere is floating above your head, and emits beautiful golden white light which bathes your entire body. Let the light penetrate and fill you completely. The golden light fills you, and surrounds you and protects you. Only beneficial things can happen to you now. You release all the negativity and resentment, which is being flushed out of your system.

Search your memory for some difficult situation that you have experienced, either in your professional or private life . . . In this situation, you have a problem with someone. The relationship is bad. An argument, a disagreement, or some other kind of aggression is taking place . . . The scene becomes clearer and clearer in your mind. Specify when it took place . . . where it happened . . . the name of the other person. You hear what is said, as well as any other sounds in the area. You re-experience the feelings you had during, and after the difficult situation . . . Maybe you associate some special odour or taste with it . . . Take your time, and try to recall everything associated with the event in your mind . . .

Take a step back and observe the scene. See it as an independent and objective observer. See yourself, standing or sitting, facing the person you're having problems with. Look at the person more carefully. Keep on seeing, hearing, and feeling the person in your mind. Enter the mind of that person. You're inside the mind of the person you're having a problem with. You see yourself through their eyes, hear yourself through their ears, feel what they feel. You see yourself facing the person, through their eyes.

Enter the thoughts of the person, asking yourself, 'What is my positive intention in opposing (say your name . . .)?' 'What don't I like about (say your name)?' 'What disturbs me? What irritates me about (your name)?' 'What is at stake for me?' 'What do I stand to gain?' 'What do I stand to lose?' 'What am I really trying to achieve by behaving this way?' Answer these questions in your mind, without forcing anything.

Pay attention to all your thoughts, even the most unusual or obscure ones, for they often carry the seeds of truth. Continue to think as if you were the other person, and ask yourself this question: 'Isn't there any other way I can reach my objective, or satisfy my need in this situation?' Try to come up with an alternative solution. You're still inside the person you're having a problem with. You see through their eyes, and perhaps you see your own face, as if you were looking at yourself in a mirror, through the other person's eyes. You're thinking for the other person, and you ask yourself, 'What else could I do to fulfil my needs?' And you try to find a second solution.

You're still thinking as if you were the person you're having trouble with. They now have two other possible solutions, aside from arguing with you or trying to dominate you. Formulate these options clearly in your mind. How do you feel in the other person's position? Do you see your adversary (you) in the same way?

Now it's time to leave the other person's body. You're an external observer once again. You still see the two people, yourself and the other, facing each other. Do you notice any change in the relationship?

It's now time to close the file and separate yourself from the persons involved. In a moment, I'm going to ask you to open your eyes. When you open your eyes, you'll be completely awake, and feel in perfect health. Your head and neck will be relaxed. You'll feel in harmony with life.

When you feel ready, become fully aware of where you are . . . of your presence here in this room . . . you feel the surface you're sitting or lying on . . . wiggle your toes, contract and relax the muscles in your legs. Move your jaw . . . Clench your fists slowly, then release them. Breathe in deeply. Stretch your whole body. When you're ready, open your eyes . . . you're completely awake, and in perfect health . . .

Before you say or do anything, take a pen and paper and write down all the information you learned during this visualization exercise.

Appendix 5: Visualization Exercise 2

To do this exercise you will need the help of another person – or you can use a tape recorder and record the text yourself.

Get comfortable in a quiet place. Don't cross your arms or legs. Close your eyes and breathe in deeply. As you breathe out, let all the tension flow out of your body. Take another deep breath. As you breathe out, rid yourself of all your mental tension. Now breathe normally, letting a feeling of total relaxation pervade your body and your mind . . .

Think of a difficult situation that you are worried about because you feel you don't have what it takes to deal with it effectively. Which quality – which inner resource – would you like to have in this situation?

Search your memory for a situation in the past where you had that inner resource. Relive the experience in your mind in as much detail as possible. Was it in a place full of light? Or was it in a dark room? If it was dark, turn the lights up higher.

Try to become aware of the quality or resource you showed at that time. Slowly close one of your hands. The more you feel the quality or resource, the tighter you clench your fist. Now open your fist slowly. Keep your eyes shut.

Try to remember another situation where you exhibited the same quality. Visualize the scene. If you can't find one, go back to the first and do it over again. Concentrate on how you felt as you demonstrated the quality, the source you are seeking. Slowly close the same hand as before. The more you feel the quality you seek, the tighter you clench your fist.

Now open your fist slowly, and let your mind relax for a moment. Close your fist again, and reinforce the positive experience you've just had. Create a mental picture of yourself in a situation in the near future where you will need this quality. Try to imagine how the difficult situation will take place. Imagine yourself in the situation, and then slowly clench your fist. Concentrate on the quality the gesture is linked to . . . the quality you need now . . .

Now come back to yourself; become aware of the surface on which you are sitting or lying; wriggle your toes, contract and relax your leg muscles; move your jaw around; clench your fists slowly. Breathe in deeply. Stretch your body. When you're ready, open your eyes. You are fully awake, and you feel in perfect health . . . Close your fist as before: you feel the quality you were seeking inside you. It was there in the past, and it's there now, ready to be used . . .

After this exercise, the simple act of closing your fists should put you in touch with the quality or resource you are seeking: courage, patience, serenity, enthusiasm, or any other quality you choose. If this doesn't happen, repeat the visualization, trying to recall a past experience where you felt the quality very strongly, and then concentrating on it as intensely as possible, while slowly clenching your fist. The more situations a quality is linked to, the stronger it becomes. Repeat the visualizations as many times as necessary to gain a firm grip on the quality you are seeking. Remember to use the same hand for only one quality at a time.

This technique is based on the unconscious association of an external physical stimulus and an internal state of mind. You can use other external stimuli; for example, pressing your thumb on any part of your body – always making sure it's the same stimulus for the same quality – or any other tactile stimulus. The link could also be triggered by an image or a sound, but they are harder to establish when doing the visualization exercise on your own, with your eyes closed.

Further Reading

Stephanie Barrat-Godefroy, *Charisma and Personal Magnetism*, Thorsons, London 1993.

Barbara Binkley and Gerald Piaget, *Dealing with Difficult People*, Educational Services Corp., Washington 1985.

Robert M. Bramson, *Coping with Difficult People*, Dell Publishing, New York 1981.

Diana Cawood, *Assertiveness for Managers*, Self Councel Press, Washington 1987.

Dr Wayne W. Dyer, *Pulling Your Own Strings*, Avon Books, New York 1978.

Les Giblin, *How You Can Have Confidence and Power in Dealing with People*, Wilshire Books, Hollywood, 1956.

Christian H. Godefroy and Stephanie Barrat, *The Power Talk System: How to Communicate Effectively*, Judy Piatkus, London 1991.

Christian H. Godefroy and Luis Robert, *The Outstanding Negotiator: How to Develop your Arguing Power*, Judy Piatkus, London 1993.

Christian H. Godefroy with David R. Steevens, *Mind Power: Use Positive Thinking to Change your Life*, Judy Piatkus, London 1993.

Suzette Haden Elgin, *The Gentle Art of Verbal Self Defense*, Dorset Press, Huntsville, 1980.

Herbert S. Kinler, *Managing Disagreement Constructively*, Crisp Publications, Los Altos 1988.

William J. Lederer, *Creating a Good Relationship*, W. W. Norton, London 1984.

Index